ISLAMIC AFRICA

ISLAMIC AFRICA

Incorporating SUDANIC AFRICA

ISLAMIC AFRICA

VOLUME 3, ISSUE 2 FALL 2012

Northwestern University Press
Evanston, Illinois

www.islamicafricajournal.org

Scope and Mission: *Islamic Africa* is a peer-reviewed, multidisciplinary, academic journal published by Northwestern University Press in collaboration with the Institute for the Study of Islamic Thought in Africa (ISITA), based at Northwestern University, Evanston, Illinois. The journal incorporates *Sudanic Africa,* retaining its focus on historical sources, bibliographies, and methodologies. *Islamic Africa* promotes interaction between scholars of Islam and Africa across all continents and across historical periods. The journal welcomes papers from the humanities and the social sciences on any aspect of Islam and Muslim life pertaining to Africa, or originating from the African continent.

Communications concerning manuscripts and editorial matters should be addressed to Prof. Scott Reese, Editor, *Islamic Africa,* Northwestern University Press, 629 Noyes Street, Evanston, IL 60208 (USA); islamicafrica@northwestern.edu. For information about submitting manuscripts, see www.islamicafricajournal.org.

Concerning advertising and subscriptions, address the Managing Editor, Gianna F. Mosser, Northwestern University Press, 629 Noyes Street, Evanston, IL 60208 (USA); islamicafrica@northwestern.edu. Electronic subscriptions can be purchased for institutions ($125) and individuals ($75) by visiting www.islamicafricajournal .org.

 ISSN 2154-0993.

Northwestern University Press acknowledges Marianne Jankowski for the interior design and Ahmad Faris for the journal logo. The copy editor for this issue was Paul Mendelson.

Contents

BOOK REVIEWS

Islamic Africa is a peer-reviewed, multidisciplinary, academic journal published by Northwestern University Press in collaboration with the Institute for the Study of Islamic Thought in Africa (ISITA), based at Northwestern University, Evanston. The journal incorporates *Sudanic Africa*, retaining its focus on historical sources, bibliographies, and methodologies. *Islamic Africa* promotes interaction between scholars of Islam and Africa across all continents and across historical periods. We welcome papers on any aspect of Islam and Muslim life pertaining to Africa and/or Africans from the humanities and the social sciences, especially those originating from the African continent.

SOURCES

Politics and Islamization in African Public Spheres

Abdulkader Tayob, UNIVERSITY OF CAPE TOWN, SOUTH AFRICA

DOI: 10.5192/215409930302139

ABSTRACT

Public Islam and Muslim publics provide a useful framework for understanding how technology and new social and political contexts have impacted discourses of religion in the public sphere. This article proposes that scholarly attention on Muslim publics has been guided by the different impacts of Wilfred Cantwell Smith and Jürgen Habermas. Smith's theory of reification has focused attention on the production of Islam(s), while Habermas's work has focused attention on the production of new values for democratic politics. Muslim publics in Africa and elsewhere point to a diversity of engagements that call for more critical reflection and analysis. This article suggests that politics and Islamization are the main preoccupations of Muslim public debates in Africa, and should be the focus of comparative and historical analysis.

Islamist politics in North Africa, the extension of shariʿah in northern Nigeria in 1999, and the constitutional review process in Kenya from the late 1990s to 2010 are some prominent examples where Muslim debates have formed an important part of African public and political life. In nonpolitical spheres the presence of symbols in mosques, schools, personal dress, and faith-based social services cannot be missed. Islam in African public life presents an extensive variety of expressions that defy easy generalization. Modernization and secularization theories hardly qualify in a context

Islamic Africa, VOL. 3, NO. 2, 2012. ISSN 2154-0993.

where religion is returning to public life. Anti-modernization theories too fail to explain religious individuals and groups that exploit modern technologies and political contexts. Although Muslims may be opposed to modernity, they are not averse to using modern tools and concepts in their religious expressions.

The concepts of public life, public Islam, and Muslim publics go part of the way in providing a framework to understand the variety of expressions that dominate Islam in Africa. As currently employed, however, they do not help in identifying major trends and preoccupations in Muslim public life. Most of the literature does not venture beyond the framework to capture some significant issues that animate these discussions. With a critical approach to the concepts of public Islam and Muslim publics, I argue that this framework of public Islam is useful but self-limiting. It is useful in pointing to the conditions under which Muslim debates in public are enabled and open to contestation, but it is limiting in that the analysis cannot take us beyond a variety of expressions of Islam.

This article proposes that Islam in public life in Africa may be identified more clearly around three major preoccupations. From the period of liberation and emancipation in the 1950s until the present, Muslim publics in Africa ranged from those that are clearly concerned with politics, those that are very specifically focused on the production and reproduction of good Muslim believers, and those concerned with civil society issues. The first may be identified as a "politics of identity" that captured the desire of Muslims to give shape and expression to national public life. This ranged from North African countries where Islam became a state religion, to countries like Nigeria, Kenya, and Tanzania where Muslims constitute a significant percentage of the population. Identity is wielded differently in each context, and calls for rigorous and comparative reflection. The second public manifestation of Islam is a continuing preoccupation with defining orthodoxy and orthopraxis for Muslim social life. In the postcolonial contexts, this continuing and renewed Islamization included the formation of ulama bodies, the proliferation of schools and mosques, and the adoption of public practices derived from the normative, textual sources of Islam. A small but widely dispersed critical discourse is a third expression of public Islam. Such a critical discourse took a legal turn in the 1990s when more liberal political changes were inaugurated in a number of African countries after the Cold War, and Islamic law was introduced in national debates and legislatures. Though relatively marginal, a critical voice on Islamic law is an equally prominent expression in African public spheres.

Public Islam and Muslim Publics

The framework of public Islam and Muslim publics is built on the insights of Wilfred Cantwell Smith, and applied to the effects and implications of the public sphere. In a series of books and articles from 1962 onward, Smith argued that Muslims (and other religions too) in the modern world were inclined to define Islam as an objectified set of ideas and practices. This reification changed the way Muslims related to religious experience.[1] The diversity of sources and voices that constituted Islamic discourses (God, the Prophet, the Companions, and the various scholarly lineages) was reduced to enunciations made in the name of Islam. *Islam* was supposed to have a view on the Bible, on women, state, and violence, displacing the deliberations of exegetes, jurists, politicians, Sufis, and other learned individuals. According to Smith, such reifications obscured the *experiences* of Muslims in such acts, beliefs, and practices. Smith considered these developments regrettable in the history of Islam.

Smith's insights are implicit in the framework of public Islam and Muslim publics that pay attention to this focus on Islam(s) in the public sphere. Salvatore's *Islam and the Political Discourse of Modernity*[2] makes explicit reference to Smith's understanding of the objectification and reification of Islam. It builds on this insight to propose that the meaning of Islam was discursively formed. It was generated through intellectuals, new and old, engaging with each other across the Mediterranean Sea. Salvatore made a distinction between a discourse of premodernity built on *dīn* (religion) and modern Islamic discourse built on Islam. His emphasis turned on the discursive nature of symbols such as *dīn* and *islam* around which a shared universe of meaning emerged. For Salvatore, religion was a product of communicative action, which led to conceptions of community, order, and cosmos.[3] In modern discourse, Islam represented a focal point for the promotion of values and practices. While Smith wanted to turn scholars away from the reifications of religion to the experiences of believers, Salvatore pointed to the complex and discursive formation of Islam.

In the next few years, Salvatore worked closely with Eickelman, Anderson, and others to suggest how the articulation of Islam was made

---

[1] W. C. Smith, *The Meaning and End of Religion* (San Francisco: Harper and Row, 1978).

[2] A. Salvatore, *Islam and the Political Discourse of Modernity*, vol. 4, International Politics of the Middle East (Reading, Eng.: Ithaca, 1997).

[3] Salvatore, *Political Discourse of Modernity*, 5.

possible in new public spheres. Their arguments about the role of Islam in public life framed research on how to examine particular instances of Islam in the public sphere. Eickelman and Salvatore have written most extensively on this topic, and brought a number of scholars together to reflect and write on "public Islam" and "Muslim publics." Public Islam referred to

> highly diverse invocations of Islam as ideas and practices that religious scholars, self-ascribed religious authorities, secular intellectuals, Sufi orders, mothers, students, workers, engineers, and many others make to civic debate and public life. In this "public" capacity, "Islam" makes a difference in configuring the politics and social life of large parts of the globe, and not just for self-ascribed religious authorities.[4]

In the preceding quote, public Islam gestures at articulations on Islam within public spaces, producing discursive spaces called Muslim publics. Through a multiplicity of new media, discussions and debates on Islam constituted such Muslim publics. These interactions produced new possibilities of both agreement and disagreement, but most important contributed to the production of shared discursive worlds. Drawing on the ideas of Dewey, Salvatore and Eickelman proposed that Muslim publics were enabled by shared standards of anticipation.[5] The role of new media was crucial in this formation, beginning with print and continuing in the era of virtual worlds. Modern media made religious texts more widely available, provided access to present one's views, and increased the possibility of sharing such ideas with others across a country or the globe. Moreover, the role of non-specialists in the production of public Islam and the constitution of Muslim publics has been repeatedly emphasized. Participation in public Islam was not limited to those who studied Islamic sciences over many years. Anyone with access to media could and did participate in the production of Muslim publics.

Public Islam and Muslim publics have been studied in diverse contexts,

---

[4] A. Salvatore and D. E. Eickelman, "Preface: Public Islam and the Common Good," in *Public Islam and the Common Good*, ed. A. Salvatore and D. E. Eickelman, Social, Economic, and Political Studies of the Middle East and Asia (Leiden: Brill, 2004), xii.

[5] A. Salvatore and D. E. Eickelman, "Muslim Publics," in *Public Islam and the Common Good*, ed. A. Salvatore and D. E. Eickelman, Social, Economic, and Political Studies of the Middle East and Asia (Leiden: Brill, 2004), 16.

inside and outside Africa. Eickelman and Anderson[6] turned to the impact of faxes, satellite television, and the Internet in the production of creolized and hybridized discourses in Arab societies. Among others, they pointed to the highly popular work of the Damascene engineer, Muhammad Shahrur, on the Qurʾan and science. Adelkhah[7] documented alternative Muslim publics within funeral rituals in Iran; Launay[8] pointed to the impact of radio and television in northern Cote d'Ivoire; Schulz[9] explored the sharing and circulation of cassettes among followers of charismatic leaders in Mali; while Allievi[10] recorded new articulations of Islam in Europe among immigrants. Muslim publics were not limited to specific political contexts, but extended in trans-national directions. Anderson explored these discursive spaces among "imagined communities" on the Internet.[11]

The interest in the public sphere among scholars of Islam coincided with its revival in eastern and southern Europe, Latin America, and southern Africa in what Casanova has called a third wave of democracy.[12] As elsewhere, this interest has been closely linked with discussions on the path of democratization as proposed in the work of Jürgen Habermas. The latter traced the history of democratization in Europe to the development of the public sphere in new political contexts. Occupied by an emerging

[6] D. E. Eickelman and J. W. Anderson, "Redefining Muslim Publics," in *New Media in the Muslim World: The Emerging Public Sphere*, ed. D. E. Eickelman and J. W. Anderson (Bloomington: Indiana University Press, 1999).

[7] F. Adelkhah, "Islam and the Common Mortal," in *Modernizing Islam: Religion in the Public Sphere in the Middle East and Europe*, ed. J. Esposito and F. Burgat (London: Hurst, 2003).

[8] R. Launay, "Spirit Media: The Electronic Media and Islam Among Dyula of Northern Cote d'Ivoire," *Africa: Journal of the International African Institute* 67, no. 3 (1997): 441–53.

[9] D. E. Schulz, "'Charisma and Brotherhood' Revisited: Mass-Mediated Forms of Spirituality in Urban Mali," *Journal of Religion in Africa: Religion and the Media* 33, no. 2 (2003): 146–71.

[10] S. Allievi, "Islam in the Public Space: Social Networks, Media and Neo-Communities," in *Muslim Networks and Transnational Communities in and Across Europe*, ed. S. Allievi and J. Nielsen (Leiden: Brill, 2003).

[11] J. W. Anderson and Y. Gonzales-Quijano, "Technological Mediation and the Emergence of Transnational Muslim Publics," in *Public Islam and the Common Good*, ed. A. Salvatore and D. E. Eickelman, Social, Economic, and Political Studies of the Middle East and Asia (Leiden: Brill, 2004); J. W. Anderson, "New Media, New Publics: Reconfiguring the Public Sphere of Islam," *Social Research* 70, no. 3 (2003): 887–906.

[12] J. Casanova, "Civil Society and Religion: Retrospective Reflections on Catholicism and Prospective Reflections on Islam," *Social Research* 68, no. 4 (2001): 1041–80.

bourgeoisie, the public sphere provided a space where notions of the common good could be articulated and debated on the basis of reason alone. Habermas closely followed the emergence of the public sphere in various political contexts in Europe, and also its disintegration under the impact of new communications and economics.[13]

Some of Habermas's analyses have been criticized, but his suggestions for democracy and politics have been followed closely. Studies in public Islam and Muslim publics have directly drawn on key issues raised by him in the promotion of democracy in Muslim societies. Thus, attention has been paid to the specific political conditions that gave rise to public spheres in modern Muslim states and societies. Soares's study pointed out how colonial policies in West Africa created new spaces for Muslim political and social activities. Islam lost its independent political capital at the royal court, but retained its relevance in social and cultural life.[14] Didier has followed similar developments in southern India during British colonialism.[15] In contrast, Salvatore and Eickelman pointed to premodern formations of public life. They stressed the continuity of public discourses in the "shared standards of anticipation" in both premodern and modern contexts.[16] The idea of the common good as the object of the public sphere in general, and Muslims in particular, is another consideration in the literature. Again, Salvatore and Eickelman edited a book on this topic, with some suggestive contributions.[17] Esposito, like many others, pointed to the multiplicity of civil voices that dominated public Islam.[18] Hefner, more

[13] J. Habermas, "On the Relations Between the Secular Liberal State and Religion," in *Political Theologies: Public Religions in a Post-Secular World*, ed. H. de Vries and L. Sullivan (New York: Fordham University Press, 2006); J. Habermas, "The Public Sphere: An Encyclopedia Article (1964)," *New German Critique* 3 (1974): 49–55.

[14] B. F. Soares, *Islam and the Prayer Economy: History and Authority in a Malian Town* (Edinburgh, Ann Arbor: Edinburgh University Press; University of Michigan Press for the International African Institute, 2005).

[15] B. J. Didier, "When Disputes Turn Public: Heresy, the Common Good, and the State in South India," in *Public Islam and the Common Good*, ed. A. Salvatore and D. E. Eickelman, Social, Economic, and Political Studies of the Middle East and Asia 95 (Leiden: Brill, 2004).

[16] A. Salvatore and D. E. Eickelman, "The Public Sphere and Muslim Identities," *European Journal of Sociology* 43 (2002): 113.

[17] A. Salvatore and D. E. Eickelman, eds. *Public Islam and the Common Good*, Social, Economic, and Political Studies of the Middle East and Asia 95 (Leiden: Brill, 2004).

[18] J. Esposito, "Islam and Civil Society," in *Modernizing Islam: Religion in the Public Sphere in the Middle East and Europe*, ed. J. Esposito and F. Burgat (London: Hurst, 2003), 90.

pointedly, referred to a deep conflict between statist and civil Islam in Indonesia.[19]

The possibility of a new politics, perhaps a democratic politics, is the subtext of most studies on public Islam and Muslim publics. In the case of Islam, the emergence of radical Islamic politics puts these studies in a particularly poignant perspective. Against a widespread Islamophobia that dominated many public spheres in the West, these studies have been at pains to suggest that the public spheres in Muslim societies are diverse in their invocations of Islam, and hold promise for new developments. Some dissenting voices in this debate have emphasized the religious values promoted within public Islam, or public Islam's global discourse that was insulated from the secular, democratic forms of public sphere debates. Ismail[20] proposed that public life is always political, but divided between public and counter-public manifestations. Going further, Hirschkind has written of Islamic counter-publics in Egypt where conformity to religious values and ideals left little room for the deliberation of common values and the common good.[21] In a different vein, Bowen has pointed to a global Islamic discourse that dominates public debates among Muslims, allowing little room for the intrusion of local values, including democratic and liberal values, in Muslim publics.[22] Both these arguments have raised important critical questions about a hasty judgment on the convergence of public Islam and a democratic public sphere in any given context. Nevertheless, the dominating influence of Habermas and the possibilities of democracy through the public sphere have dominated academic literature.

The political questions driven by Habermas's thesis of democratization have obscured the concept of reified Islam in the framework of public Islam and Muslim publics. Since Salvatore, discussions on public Islam and Muslim publics have implicitly accepted Smith's analysis, and have been preoccupied by how "Islam(s)" were articulated, extended, or restricted. Muslim representation of Islam has been assumed from Smith, and applied

---

[19] R. W. Hefner, "Public Islam and the Problem of Democratization," *Sociology of Religion* 62, no. 4 (2001): 491–514.

[20] S. Ismail, "Islamism, Re-Islamization and the Fashioning of Muslim Selves: Refiguring the Public Sphere," *Muslim World Journal of Human Rights* 4, no. 1 (2007): 1–21.

[21] C. Hirschkind, "Civic Virtue and Religious Reason: An Islamic Counterpublic," *Cultural Anthropology* 16, no. 1 (2001): 3–34; C. Hirschkind, *The Ethical Soundscape: Cassette Sermons and Islamic Counterpublics* (New York: Columbia University Press, 2006).

[22] J. R. Bowen, "Beyond Migration: Islam as a Transnational Public Space," *Journal of Ethnic and Migration Studies* 30, no. 5 (2003): 879–94.

to a variety of contexts, including the Internet. More specifically, studies have emphasized the discursive formation of Islam, and its representation in public life. As Muslim invested their efforts in the real meaning of Islam, scholarly studies similarly restricted their attention to the "enunciations of Islam." They have been satisfied to identify the variety of Islams, adding more nuances to the many ways in which Islam was articulated anew. Islam was in a variety of ways discursively constituted through print, then radio, followed by television, and now new media.

The discursive formation of religion in modern contexts cannot be denied, nor the impact of liberalizing politics, modern technology, and increased access to information. However, some distinctive issues that have preoccupied Muslim publics in various Muslim societies, or within the global *ummah*, need to be recognized. The preoccupation with "islam" as the major symbol and target of Muslim debate has obscured specific deliberations on values, ethics, and rituals. Many Muslims do indeed express their views in the name of Islam. However, closer attention reveals that Islam in public life is preoccupied with identifiable issues that merit greater attention. This article thus proposes that a number of studies on Muslim publics and public Islam in Africa reveal that the issues discussed can be more clearly identified. While the expressions may be framed in the name of Islam, closer attention reveals very distinct debates around politics and religion. The following survey draws on a limited set of examples across the continent, but suggests ideas for further reflection and critical scrutiny of what is going on inside and through public Islam and Muslim publics.

Politics of Identity

The politics of identity in Europe and North America has generally focused on the nation-state and multiculturalism. Most reflections on the politics of identity have been associated with liberal politics and the accommodation of culture and identity. Philosophers and political theorists disagree on the value of culture/identity in the formation of policy, political values, and good citizens.[23] In some critical theory, the politics of identity has also been seen as a replacement or substitute for class in political

[23] C. Taylor, *Multiculturalism and "the Politics of Recognition": An Essay by Charles Taylor with Commentary by Amy Gutmann, Steven C. Rockefeller, Michael Walzer, Susan Wolf* (Princeton, N.J.: Princeton University Press, 1992); S. Benhabib, *The Claims of Culture: Equality and Diversity in the Global Era* (Princeton, N.J.: Princeton University Press,

participation and analysis. Such critique points to the emergence of new forms of political participation since the 1960s.[24] Both these issues and debates do not sufficiently represent the politics of identity in African public spheres, let alone Islam and the public sphere. In the following, I suggest a number of contexts where religious symbols and identities have preoccupied politics and public debates in African Muslim societies. This review suggests fundamental disagreements on politics and political cultures that feed into deliberations in Muslim publics.

I begin with religious nationalism, which may be identified as a politics of identity. Hastings, in particular, has questioned the secular framing of nationalism in the literature, pointing out how central a role religion has played in the formation of modern nations.[25] In Africa, religious nationalist debates have played a role in public sphere debates and discussions, and also conflicts. North Africa represents one version of an Islamic nationalist discourse. From the Moroccan king to Egypt's socialist, democratic republic, Islam was declared the state religion, and each of the countries pursued a path of modernization and state-building that included a reformist interpretation of Islam.[26] The roots of this reformist/nationalist discourse can be traced to the nineteenth century when personalities like Amīr ʿAbd al-Qādir al-Jazāʾirī (d. 1883) and Khayr al-Dīn al-Tunisī (d. 1890) loomed large in a reformist tradition that resisted European colonialism and imperialism. They were followed by others in the twentieth century, centered around the impact and influence of the Egyptian Muḥammad ʿAbduh (d. 1905). Reformists advocated a return to the original teaching of Islam as a path to modernization. Moreover, they proposed that Islam in essence was compatible with modernization (and not Westernization) as inaugurated in Europe.[27] This particular understanding of Islam was absorbed into the

2002); W. Kymlicka, *Multicultural Citizenship: A Liberal Theory of Minority Rights* (Oxford: Clarendon, 1995).

[24] J. W. Scott, "Multiculturalism and the Politics of Identity," in *The Identity in Question*, ed. J. Rajchman (New York: Routledge, 1995).

[25] A. Hastings, *The Construction of Nationhood: Ethnicity, Religion and Nationalism* (Cambridge, Eng.: Cambridge University Press, 1997).

[26] A. Christelow, "Ritual, Culture and Politics of Islamic Reformism in Algeria," *Middle Eastern Studies* 23, no. 3 (1987): 255–74; L. C. Brown, "The Islamic Reformist Movement in North Africa," *Journal of Modern African Studies* 2, no. 1 (1964): 55–63.

[27] N. H. Abu Zeid, "The Modernisation of Islam or the Islamisation of Modernity," in *Cosmopolitanism, Identity and Authenticity in the Middle East*, ed. Roel Meijer (Surrey, Eng.: Curzon, 1999).

national identity of the new states. It provided an important justification for modernization. Like other modern ideologies, reformist Islam monopolized the definition of religion, and explicitly proscribed other non-state political parties and movements founded in the name of Islam.

Islamist movements from the 1970s challenged the legitimacy of these states, and often precisely on their religious foundations or lack thereof. The most widely studied of these movements has been the Muslim Brotherhood in Egypt, and the most successful at the polls prior to the Arab Spring of 2011 was the Projet de Programme du Front Islamique du Salut (FIS), a coalition of Islamic parties and movements in Algeria that won the first round of national elections in 1990. The National Islamic Front in the Sudan, under the leadership of Ḥasan al-Turābī, is another example of an Islamist movement founded on Islamic symbols and values.[28] Islamists are deeply divided among themselves on tactics and philosophies, but they generally offered a new form of politics and public life that, in their view, was more committed to the traditions of Islam. In terms of public life, Islamist groups and individuals debated the place of Islam in state and society. Issues of identity and authenticity were the central preoccupations of this public discourse. Postcolonial states were accused of abandoning Islam, and drawing on models and inspiration from Europe. The postcolonial states, according to Islamists, were promoting public life in flagrant contradiction with the society's cultural traditions. The failures of the postcolonial states, despotic rule and dependence on support from Western countries, reinforced their alienation from a public debate that was increasingly turning to religion. By the time the Arab revolutions swept across the North Africa and the Middle East in 2011, Islamist groups had become the most prominent political groups in these countries.

Religious nationalism in the form of an explicit state ideology did not play such a dominant role in all African societies. But this did not mean the absence of religion and religious discourse in political and public life. Muslim-majority countries in sub-Saharan Africa created more explicitly secular (laic) states with various degrees of co-optation of and legitimacy from religion. Countries like Mali, Senegal, Niger, and Chad that inherited a political culture from the French, and also Somalia with a history of Italian colonialism, promoted a strict separation of religion and politics. With some exceptions, most of the Islamic groups in these countries accepted

---

[28] E. E. Shahin, *Political Ascent: Contemporary Islamic Movements in North Africa* (Boulder, Colo.: Westview, 1997).

this arrangement. On the other hand, countries with a history of British colonial rule were not as decisive on secularism. In some of these countries, Muslims and Christians engaged in a constant competition over the symbolic identity of the state. Such politics included a close watch over the religious identities of those in power, a dominant religious identity among citizens, and intra- and inter-religious conflict and competition. The public sphere dimension of this contestation may be clarified when we look at some examples.

In northern Nigeria, colonial rule attempted to preserve a semblance of continuity from the past. In particular, the descendants of the great Uthman dan Fodio (1754–1817) were nurtured and protected by the British through indirect rule. By the time of independence, this leadership had become very powerful and wished to preserve its position in the new state. Ahmadu Bello, governor of northern Nigeria from 1959 to 1966, played a dominant role in laying the foundation for this leadership in post-independent Nigerian politics. His political ambition was closely connected to the construction of a particular Nigerian Muslim identity in a number of ways. His own political party, the Northern People's Congress, would be the home for a national Nigerian Islamic identity. Bello also formed a *national* religious body, Jamaat Nasr al-Islam (Society for the Support of Islam), in 1962. He also tried to found a new Sufi order, Usmaniyya, to supersede or bring together rival Sufi groups of the Tijaniyya and Qadariyya. More significant, he supported a rising Islamic preacher, Abu Bakr Gumi (d. 1992), to lead this Islamic political project. Gumi was appointed grand kadi (judge), and later invited to present a series of sermons in the Sultan Bello Mosque.[29] When Bello was assassinated in 1965, the search for both Muslim unity and hegemony on the national front did not die with him.[30] He had laid the foundation of a politics of identity in Nigeria that promoted a singular Muslim national purpose. This identity was opposed to a perceived Christian dominance in postcolonial Nigeria.

[29] Sheikh A. Gumi and I. A. Tsiga, *Where I Stand?* (Ibadan, Nigeria: Spectrum Books, 2001).

[30] J. O. Hunwick, "An African Case Study of Political Islam," *Annals of the American Academy of Political and Social Science* 524 (1992): 143–55; R. Loimeier, "Islamic Reform and Political Change: The Example of Abubakar Gumi and the Yan Izala Movement in Northern Nigeria," in *African Islam and Islam in Africa*, ed. E. E. Rosander and D. Westerlund (London: Hurst, 1997).

In comparison with Nigeria, Muslim identity has a more equivocal and complex place in East African public life. Prior to independence, the island of Zanzibar witnessed the emergence of Swahili nationalism with a strong Muslim identity. But the contradictions were too deep between the different classes and ethnicities that constituted Swahili identity, and the general current in the region tended toward secular nationalist leadership. Moreover, Islam was associated with slavery and Zanzibari Arab colonialism within nationalist circles. Glassman rightly contends that African and lower-class Muslims on the East African coast also rejected Arab hegemony.[31] The Zanzibari revolution of 1964 put an end to any ambition of Islamic identity in the body politic of East African states.[32]

Religion was not completely banished from East African politics. Immediately after independence, the relationship between government and Muslims was guided through state-recognized bodies. Both Muslim and Christian groups were registered and recognized for partnership with the state. When Muslims were too deeply divided among themselves, state-sponsored and state-supported national councils were formed and recognized in each of the countries: Kenya's Supreme Council of Kenya Muslims (SUPKEM; est. 1973), Tanzania's Baraza Kuu la Waislamu (Higher Islamic Council), Uganda's National Association for the Advancement of Muslims (est. 1964) and National Muslim Council (1965), and the Muslim Association in Malawi. These organizations worked with ruling governments and parties, irrespective of their political philosophies and ideologies.[33] Later both Muslim and Christian political leaders in the region sought more support and legitimacy from religion to support their policies and their long-term rule. Idi Amin's infamous rule is well known for its ostensible support for Muslims in Uganda. What is equally significant is how Daniel Arap Moi extended his

[31] J. Glassman, "Stolen Knowledge: Struggles for Popular Islam on the Swahili Coast, 1870–1963," in *Islam in East Africa: New Sources (Archives, Manuscripts and Written Historical Sources: Oral History, Archaeology)*, ed. B. S. Amoretti, International Colloquium (Rome, December 2–4, 1999) (Rome: Herder Editrice le Libreria, 2001).

[32] M. F. Lofchie, *Zanzibar: Background to Revolution* (Princeton, N.J.: Princeton University Press, 1965).

[33] F. Constantin, "Muslims and Politics: The Attempts to Create Muslim National Organisations in Tanzania, Uganda and Kenya," in *Religion and Politics in East Africa: The Period Since Independence*, ed. H. B. Hansen and M. Twaddle, Eastern African Studies (London: James Curry, 1995); J. Haynes, "Islam and Democracy in East Africa," *Democratization* 13, no. 3 (2006): 490–507.

rule of Kenya from 1978 to 2002 with a Christian symbolism that inscribed the nation.[34]

Oded and Haynes have argued that this accommodation between autocratic postcolonial regimes and religion was shaken by the inauguration of multiparty politics in the early 1990s.[35] A more assertive approach to the status quo emerged within Muslim public debates and activities in the region. In Kenya, the Islamic Party of Kenya (IPK) sought registration under new party laws, and put ideas of Islamic politics in the national debate. Supporters of the party demanded greater representation of Islam in the nation, and wanted laws of shariʿah extended to non-family matters. Aggrieved by their marginalization in Moi's regime, some Muslims turned to the IPK and other similar religio-political bodies. Generally, they contested the legitimacy of national Muslim bodies, and promoted alternative forms of religious and social life.

Symbols and identities in the public sphere, then, have been important features of African Muslim debates. They were part of a modernist reformist discourse in North African state ideologies, and were also present in contestations over the representation of religion in the national politics of East Africa. Public debates were preoccupied with the place and meaning of religion and its symbols in politics and statecraft. In relation to Islam, alternative Muslim discourses challenged agreed settlements in the political sphere entrenched after independence. Islamists in North Africa challenged what they called the secularist and Western frameworks of the status quo, while Islamists in East Africa challenged the legitimacy of national representative bodies established in the 1960s and 1970s. In short, Muslim publics regularly inserted religious identity into public and political spheres in Africa. Consequently, research on public Islam and Muslim publics ought to analyze these deliberations in terms of political theory and culture.

Islamization of the Public Sphere

Debate on the role and place of Islam in state and government is not the only preoccupation of Muslim publics; Islamization has been another

[34] A. Mazrui, "Ethnicity and Pluralism: The Politicization of Religion in Kenya," *Journal of Muslim Minority Affairs* 14, no. 1 (1993): 191-201.

[35] A. Oded, *Islam and Politics in Kenya* (London: Lynne Rienner Publishers, 2000); Haynes, "Islam and Democracy in East Africa."

prominent feature. Islamization here refers to the greater extent to which the norms and symbols of Islamic law, theology, and mysticism are promoted and then adopted in private and public life. Muslims are urged to transform their personal behavior, home, cuisine, politics, and social activities in conformity with such norms and values. The literature on public Islam and Muslim publics has shown how this Islamization has been promoted in modern societies.

Scholarship on public Islam and Muslim publics has particularly reflected on the impact of technology and mass education on Islamic debates. Modern forms of communication from printing to the Internet have facilitated this Islamization. Ideas and trends moved quickly from one place of the world to another through mass communication systems. Mass schooling has increased rates of literacy to access these texts. Schools and associations were founded, and supported Islamization in diverse ways. Where previously the meaning of Islam was restricted to the articulation of scholars steeped in learning, now it was expanded to include "secular intellectuals, Sufi orders, mothers, students, workers, engineers, and many others."[36]

The literature has stressed the possibilities of new values emerging from new classes of individuals participating in the production of Islam. The literature, however, has not sufficiently reflected on the power of religious elites to use modern technology, and modern public spaces, to limit innovation in practices and values. While scholars on public Islam have focused on the *possibilities* of the public sphere, they have not sufficiently taken note of the support given to traditional forms of religious norms in modern contexts. In fact, religious leaders (ulama) have used the opportunities provided by the modern state, and modern technology, to emphasize the obligation of Muslims to live according to the norms of the original texts of Islam. A select review of cases in African countries points to the proliferation of institutions and practices that promoted the continuity of beliefs and practices from the past.

In Nigeria, Abu Bakr Gumi did not only serve Bello's political interests; he was also influential in the promotion of religious behavior and conformity to the shariʿah and theology in the public sphere. Like other reformists, he campaigned for Muslim public practices to be reformed in terms of the Qurʾan and sunna of the Prophet. In the Nigerian context, such reformist ideas were directed against the vast influence of Tijaniyya

[36] Salvatore and Eickelman, "Preface: Public Islam and the Common Good," xii.

and Qadiriyya Sufi networks.[37] Similarly in East Africa, reformist (*salafī*) teachers and students insisted that Swahili Muslims abandon cultural practices that did not strictly and literally conform to the texts of Islam.[38] Religious scholars, Sufi sheikhs, *mallams*, and ulama were organizing themselves in various ways, and advocating some religious reform or another. And, without exception, they have become very prominent in almost every African country.

Moosa and Vahed have documented and studied the Islamization of the public sphere in the minority context of South African Muslims of South Asian origin.[39] At the height of the repression unleashed by the apartheid state in the 1960s and 1970s, Islamic public life was being slowly transformed. This change was led mainly by religious leaders who graduated from the seminaries of India, and returned to take control over mosques and ritual spaces in the country.[40] Moreover, a sectarian conflict between Deobandis and Barelvis played itself out in these sites. Deobandis, in particular, criticized the folk and family traditions inherited from India with regard to marriage rites, prophetic celebration rituals, funeral traditions, and traditional practices. The Tablighi Jamaat, as a close ally of the Deobandis, popularized these changes through a very effective mass movement. The Barelvis, or Sunnis, as they prefer to be called, also derived their inspiration from India. However, they championed folk Islamic practices, and accused the Deobandis of innovations. The clash between the Deobandis and Barelvis led to major conflicts in mosques and homes among family members, and eventually a death at a mosque in 1987 in Azaadville near Johannesburg. This contest laid the foundation for extensive public teaching, the proliferation of texts, and later extensive use of media (radio), leading to increased awareness of Islamic religious obligations. Select verses from the Qurʾan and statements of the Prophet Muhammad were popularized in pamphlets, in books, on radio, and on the

---

[37] Loimeier, "Abubakar Gumi and the Yan Izala Movement."

[38] S. Turner, "'These Young Men Show No Respect for Local Customs'—Globalization and Islamic Revival in Zanzibar," *Journal of Religion in Africa* 39, no. 3 (2009): 237–61.

[39] E. Moosa, "Worlds 'Apart': Tablighi Jama'at in South Africa under Apartheid, 1963–1993," *Journal for Islamic Studies* 17 (1997): 28–48; G. Vahed, "Contesting 'Orthodoxy': The Tablighi-Sunni Conflict among South African Muslims in the 1970s and 1980s," *Journal of Muslim Minority Affairs* 23, no. 2 (2003): 313–34.

[40] A. I. Tayob, *Islam in South Africa: Mosques, Imams and Sermons* (Gainesville: University of South Florida Press, 1999).

Internet. This conflict did not lead to new public values of Islam, but to the entrenchment of values and discourses around the Qurʾan and sunna of the Prophet.

Janson has similarly studied the Islamization of the public sphere in Gambia, which gives a different perspective to reform in a majoritarian Muslim society. She has documented the rise of the Tablighi Jamaat, with strong support from South Africa, among young unemployed men and women.[41] As in South Africa, a reformist understanding of Islam took shape against a Sufi-oriented epistemology which included claims to esoteric access to knowledge, and support for traditional practices at graveyards and commemoration sites. Janson argued that the two approaches did not apparently lead to any single dominating approach.[42] Supported by international trends, alternative esoteric traditions and cultures were, however, pushed to the margins or the background. She also noted the very explicit support given for Islamic debates by the president of the country, Yahya Jammeh, since 1994. Reformist groups successfully promoted public religious observance in societies.

Moving our focus to institutions that favor Islamization, we can look at education (*taʿlīm*) as a central component in the Islamization of the public sphere. Education takes place informally through private teacher-pupil relations, and also through established schools. The scholarly traditions in West Africa around Malikism, and in East Africa around Shafiʾism, have played a significant role in the ubiquity and strength of Islamization in the public sphere. The Hanafis and Shafiʾis in South Africa have also founded seminaries modeled on Indian traditions.[43] These scholarly traditions have been preserved within mystical orders, as in Senegal, or without them, as in Kenya. Often, as in Nigeria, Kenya, and Zanzibar, such traditions are maintained through a legally sanctioned system of shariʾah courts. And most of them maintained a continuous link with their counterparts outside Africa through educational sojourns, mystical lineages, and book

---

[41] M. Janson, "Roaming About for God's Sake: The Upsurge of the Tabligh Jama'at in the Gambia," *Journal of Religion in Africa* 35, no. 4 (2005): 450–81.

[42] M. Janson, "'We Are All the Same, Because We All Worship God': The Controversial Case of a Female Saint in the Gambia," *Africa* 76, no. 4 (2006): 502–25.

[43] D. Reetz, "The Tablīghī Madrassas in Lenasia and Azaadville: Local Players in the Global 'Islamic Field,'" in *Muslim Schools and Education in South Africa and Europe*, ed. Abdulkader I. Tayob et al. (Münster: Waxmann Verlag, 2011); M. K. Sayed, "The Shifting World of South African Madrasahs, 1973–2008" (M.A. thesis, University of Cape Town, 2010).

transfers. The teachers and scholars run basic schooling for children all over African Muslim communities. They also provide the basic knowledge base of religious education for new Muslim schools. The vitality and success of these schools has ensured a greater adherence to the textual traditions of Islam.

In addition to these religious schools and networks, Islamic schools have been founded by both governments and religious communities to promote some form of modern education among Muslims. These schools combined modern scientific education and religious socialization. In many countries, such religious schools were founded in the context of mass education projects by postcolonial states in order to create new citizens, professionals, and leaders. Muslims had at first resisted such schooling due to their association with a colonizer who was also a Christian. Later, however, many Muslims themselves introduced schools when they recognized the importance and value of modern education. The Yoruba in Nigeria were probably the first African Muslims that took this approach.[44] Brenner has studied these highly organized schools in Mali where the secular state's refusal to provide for religious education prompted students of Arabic to found their own schools. In all these institutions, the promulgation of Islamic norms and mores continues in spite of the secular ideology of the state or the broader objective of the schools.[45] Such new Muslim schools provided another site where the norms and values of Islamic texts were promoted.[46]

Of course, this greater conformity to religious practices and values should not ignore the profound changes concealed by the apparent continuities. Islamization conceals more complex changes within the societies, one of which may be illustrated. Writing on reformist trends in Kenya and

---

[44] S. Reichmuth, "Education and the Growth of Religious Associations Among Yoruba Muslims—the Ansaar-Ul-Deen Society on Nigeria," *Journal of Religion in Africa* 26, no. 4 (1996): 365–405; S. Reichmuth, "New Trends in Islamic Education in Nigeria: A Preliminary Account," *Die Welt des Islams,* New Series 29, no. 1/4 (1989): 41–60.

[45] L. Brenner, *Controlling Knowledge: Religion, Power and Schooling in a West African Muslim Society* (London: Hurst, 2000).

[46] A. Tayob et al., eds., *Muslim Schools and Education in South Africa and Europe*, Religionen im Dialog (Münster: Waxmann, 2011); G. Starret, *Putting Islam to Work: Education, Politics, and Religious Transformation in Egypt* (Berkeley: University of California Press, 1998); S. Reichmuth, "A Regional Centre of Islamic Learning in Nigeria: Ilorin and Its Influence on Yoruba Islam," in *Madrasa: La transmission du savoir dans le monde musulman*, ed. N. Grandin and M. Gaborieu (Paris: XP Editions Arguments, 1997).

the East African coast since the nineteenth century, Seeseman has shown how the content of what is identified and thus targeted as African has changed. In particular, the *mawlid* celebrations in honor of the birth of the Prophet are attacked as remnants and relics of African customs and traditions. And yet these practices were introduced in Africa in the nineteenth century from Yemen as quintessentially Islamic traditions.[47] It seems, then, that processes of identifying what is African and what is not are not settled once and for all, but are open to further contestation. More generally, Seeseman has shown how Islamization conceals deep anxieties about identity that can be traced back to social and political changes.

Islamization throughout Africa indicates greater access to the sources of Islam, populational literacy, and conformity to the textual traditions of Islam. This process of greater Islamization has been going on for a long time, and perhaps bears witness to what Sanneh and Fisher have called an internal logic within Islamic tradition that began long before the European colonial encounter. As the texts and sources of Islam are made available to more Muslims, there is a slow but inexorable trend to greater conformity.[48] Folk traditions are thereby marginalized as the reformist discourse and logic holds sway. In the context of Africa, so-called African traditions are identified for removal from the public sphere.[49] This range of acceptable and consensual *public* practice should be acknowledged as a feature of public Islam and Muslim publics in modern states. Contrary to expectation, the public sphere is not a space for new values and deliberations. Rather, technology and public spaces are the foundations on which renewed traditions of Islamic theology and orthopraxis are entrenched.

The Islamization of the public sphere is clearly a process where Muslims in modern publics are accessing the texts of Islam in diverse ways. Through educational movements, critical argumentation over orthodoxy,

---

[47] R. Seeseman, "African Islam or Islam in Africa? Evidence from Kenya," in *The Global Worlds of the Swahili: Interfaces of Islam, Identity and Space in 19th and 20th-Century East Africa*, ed. R. Seeseman and R. Loimeier (Berlin: Lit Verlag, 2006).

[48] H. J. Fisher, "The Juggernaut's Apologia: Conversion to Islam in Black Africa," *Africa: Journal of the International African Institute* 55, no. 2 (1985): 153–73; L. Sanneh, "Translatability in Islam and in Christianity in Africa: A Thematic Approach," in *Religion in Africa: Experience and Expression*, ed. Thomas D. Blakely et al. (London: James Curry, 1994).

[49] E. E. Rosander, "Introduction: The Islamization of 'Tradition' and 'Modernity,'" in *African Islam and Islam in Africa: Encounters Between Sufis and Islamists*, ed. D. Westerlund and E. E. Rosander (London: Hurst and Company in cooperation with the Nordic Africa Institute, Uppsala, Sweden, 1997).

and orthopraxis, Muslims actors are adopting what they consider to be the original meaning of Islam. Their answers are diverse, but they seem to be agreeing on a framework which supports conformity to the literal traditions of the past. Innovations are explicitly shunned, and a new purity claimed in the literal meaning of the texts of Islam. A closer look at Islamization reveals some complex formations, but the Islamization itself is unmistakable.

Critical Activism

Critical activism is another distinguishable preoccupation of Muslim publics in Africa. Such activists are usually overshadowed by identity politics and waves of Islamization, but they form an important feature of public life in African societies. Critical discourse first appeared in national politics when Muslims throughout Africa participated in liberation movements and post-independent reconstructive programs. These ranged from the elaborate political philosophy of Mahmud Muhammad Taha (d. 1983) and the Republican Party in Sudan, to Nigeria's Aminu Kanu in the 1950s who opposed the ruling Muslim aristocracy, to activism against apartheid South Africa in the 1980s.[50] Since the 1990s, critical activists have focused on Islamic law, and challenged the effects of Islamization on national levels. While Muslims demanded the Islamization of the legislature, critical activists have challenged the forms and values of such shariʿah-based legal solutions. Some examples of both political and legal activists will illustrate the place of such debates in African Muslim publics.

At the time of independence, Bello's political opinions were not the only options for Muslims in Nigeria. His Northern People's Congress opposed and defeated another prominent politician who had a different perspective on the role of Islam and its traditional leaders in northern Nigeria. Aminu Kano (1920–1983) was born into a religious scholarly family, became a schoolteacher, and then went on to lead the Northern Elements Progressive Union. He opposed indirect rule pursued in northern Nigeria during colonialism, which included both the British and local religio-political

[50] F. Esack, "Three Islamic Strands in the South Africa Struggle for Justice," *Third World Quarterly* 10, no. 2 (1988): 473–98; H. A. Jack, "Malam Aminu Kano: A Profile," *Africa Today* 6, no. 4 (1959): 6–10; M. Mahmoud, "Mahmud Muhammad Taha's Second Message of Islam and His Modernist Project," in *Islam and Modernity: Muslim Intellectuals Respond*, ed. John Cooper et al. (London: I. B. Taurus, 2000).

aristocracy of which Bello was a part.[51] After independence, Kano supported a politics that was not founded on a common identity of Muslims in Nigeria. It was based on social values shared with other Nigerians. Similar developments may be identified in a number of other countries in Africa shortly after independence.[52]

More recently, critical discussions on Islamic law have challenged the received wisdom on the shape and meaning of Islamic law in contemporary contexts. Such a discourse has generally appealed to the greater objectives (*maqāṣid*) of the shariʿah than its specific rules. African Muslims have been part of, if not taken the lead in, these debates on a global level.[53] They have pointed repeatedly to the changing context of contemporary social relations in which Muslims live. As a result, they have argued that shariʾah rules, even if derived directly from the foundation texts, should be open to revision. Abdullahi an-Naʿim is one of the few Muslim intellectuals to propose that Muslims should accept the framework of a secular state, while the public space becomes a space free for the articulation of religion.[54] An-Naiʿim developed these ideas in a context when Islamist politics were embarking on a variety of political projects to Islamize state and society. He pointed out that such policies, if not subject to revision, would deprive women and non-Muslims of their citizenship rights. Other activists have interrogated the meaning and implications of Islamic law, and advocated Islamic legal reforms in diverse forms.

A closer look at South Africa presents an example of such a critical voice. The democratic dispensation inaugurated at the end of apartheid in South Africa ratified one of the most progressive constitutions in the world. It included numerous cultural rights, one of them being the right to marriage systems in terms of a cultural tradition. However, it also insisted that such rights would be governed by the general principles of the

---

[51] Jack, "Malam Aminu Kano"; R. Loimeier, *Islamic Reform and Political Change in Northern Nigeria*, Series in Islam and Society in Africa (Evanston, Ill.: Northwestern University Press, 1997).

[52] J. M. Allman, "'Hewers of Wood, Carriers of Water': Islam, Class, and Politics on the Eve of Ghana's Independence," *African Studies Review* 34, no. 2 (1991): 1–26; Mahmoud, "Mahmud Muhammad Taha's Second Message."

[53] D. L. Johnston, "Maqāṣid al-Sharīʿa: Epistemology and Hermeneutics of Muslim Theologies of Human Rights," *Die Welt des Islams* 47, no. 2 (2007): 149–87.

[54] A. A. al-Na'im, *Toward an Islamic Reformation: Civil Liberties, Human Rights, and International Law*, Contemporary Issues in the Middle East (Syracuse, N.Y.: Syracuse University Press, 1990).

constitution (the Bill of Rights).[55] South African Muslims have debated the particular content and form of legislation enabled by the clause. The contentious point has revolved around the compatibility between Muslim personal law and the Bill of Rights. The majority of Muslims believed that a compromise with the constitution was inherently impossible. In contrast to the human construction of the constitution, Muslim personal law was divine in origin. Its provisions, they insisted, could not be subject to compromise and historical conditioning.[56] Women's interest groups and progressive Islamic organizations disagreed, and insisted that Islamic law was always a product of interpretation. Moreover, they argued that the constitution should be read in its entirety. For them, the crux of the constitutional provision for cultural and religiously sanctioned marriages was subject to "other provisions of the Constitution" (Clause 15.3b). This constitutional clause required an interpretation of Islamic law that would not be disadvantageous to women.

The leading and most articulate spokesperson for this new interpretation of Muslim personal law was Ebrahim Moosa. In both academic and newspaper articles, he has put forward the idea that the shariʿah should be distinguished from *fiqh* (positive law). The latter was mainly produced by scholars whose contextual interpretations need no longer be valid in modern times.[57] With this distinction, Moosa argued that *fiqh* could be reconstructed in terms of the constitution. Moosa taught and inspired students and activists to revisit traditional issues in Islamic law. A strong voice emerged for a significant reformulation of Islamic law. Even when Moosa moved to the United States, this critical activist voice remained vigilant and creative, and was eventually taken over by a number of Muslim lawyers and feminist activists. Under pressure from the Women's Legal Centre, the Minister of Justice presented a bill in 2009. This reopened

[55] Clause 3 or Article 15 (Chapter 2) of the Constitution of South Africa 1996 reads as follows: "This section does not prevent legislation recognising, (i) marriages concluded under any tradition, or a system of religious, personal or family law; or (ii) systems of personal and family law under any tradition, or adhered to by persons professing a particular religion. Recognition in terms of paragraph (a) must be consistent with this section and the other provisions of the Constitution" (http://www.info.gov.za/documents/constitution/1996/96cons2.htm#15).

[56] See wwwserver.law.wits.ac.za/salc/salc.html.

[57] E. Moosa, "Prospects of Muslim Law in South Africa: A History and Recent Developments," in *Yearbook of Islamic and Middle Eastern Law, Volume 3,* ed. E. Cotran and C. Mallat (London: Kluwer Law International, 1996).

a critical debate over the meaning and purpose of Islamic family law in public life among Muslims in South Africa. Whatever the final result, a critical voice on Islamic law has become part of the South African Muslim public.[58]

Critical Islamic voices have been mobilized and galvanized in other countries. They have been heard in the extension of shariᶜah in northern Nigerian states since 1999. Judgments passed by courts in cases of adultery have been challenged in higher courts, but also within Muslim public debates.[59] In Egypt, the parliament passed the so-called Khulᶜ Law in 2000, which basically gave women the right to apply for a no-fault divorce without the consent of the husband.[60] Importantly, the new law was supported by legal activists and women's groups in Cairo. In 2004, Morocco passed a Reformed Family Code after years of intense public debate. Human rights activists demanded more rights for women in marriages, while opponents saw the 1956 Family Code as the centerpiece of a nationalist tradition.[61] These examples clearly illustrated the difference between a national Islamic identity and a critical engagement with Islamic law. More important, critical discussions became part of Muslim publics.

It is true to say such critical voices do not always enjoy a great deal of popular support. However, as these few examples show, they are part of a vibrant public debate, and have been effective in being heard within societies and political and legal circles. Moreover, some of these critical discussions have even made an impact within Islamist movements in Tunisia, Egypt, and South Africa.[62] And they may play a bigger role still in the wake of the Arab Spring revolutions of 2011.

---

[58] A. Tayob, ed., *Muslim Marriages in South Africa: From Constitution to Legislation: Papers Presented at Muslim Marriages Workshop, Saturday 22 May 2010, Capetonian Hotel* (Cape Town: Centre for Contemporary Islam, UCT, 2011).

[59] A. Imam and S. Medar-Gould, "Please Stop the International Amina Lawal Protest Letter Campaigns," http://www.wluml.org/node/1025.

[60] O. Arabi, "The Dawning of the Third Millennium on Shari'a: Egypt's Law No. 1 of 2000, or Women May Divorce at Will," *Arab Law Quarterly* 16, no. 1 (2001): 2–21.

[61] J. L. M. Dieste, "'Demonstrating Islam': The Conflict of Text and the *Mudawwana* Reform in Morocco," *The Muslim World* 99 (2009): 134–54.

[62] A. Tayob, "Race, Ideology, and Islam in Contemporary South Africa," in *Islam in World Cultures: Comparative Perspectives*, ed. R. Michael Feener (Santa Barbara, Calif.: ABC CLIO, 2004); R. D. Lee, "Tunisian Intellectuals: Responses to Islamism," *Journal of North African Studies* 13, no. 2 (2008): 157–73; S. Akhavi, "Sunni Modernist Theories of Social

Conclusion

This article has made a plea to go beyond the framework of public Islam and Muslim publics to examine the debates within such formations. It has argued that the concepts of public Islam and Muslim publics are too closely tied to Smith's thesis of the reification of Islam. Such a conceptual framework limits the analysis to the meanings and representations of Islam in a variety of contexts. The goal of analysis seems limited to how new and interesting discourses are invented and inscribed for Islam. As a result, the public construction of Islam is the center of analysis. These concepts are useful framing devices to identify the form of discourse in public, but they are not sufficient for locating the particular values and practices that guide and animate them. They point to the discursive nature of Muslim debates, but tend to overlook the specific arguments pursued in the name of Islam. In this paper, I have shown the preoccupation of Muslim publics with politics and religion as represented in a sample survey of the literature. Future research should pursue the effects of Muslim publics in greater detail and depth.

Taking my specific identification of identity politics, Islamization, and critical activism as central features of Muslim publics, some general remarks may be ventured beyond the framing of Muslim publics. I propose that public Islam and Muslim publics are mainly engaged in politics; they are not merely articulating an expression of Islam. Muslim identity is very clearly political, and so is the critical activism committed to the kind of secular state clearly advocated by an-Naʾim. The focus on Islamization of the public sphere may also be classified as a form of politics. Forms of Islamization vary from a deep-seated hostility of the secular state, to a large measure of indifference or convenient accommodation. Such Islamization draws on the long history of Islamic values in the public sphere that can be traced to the beginning of Islam. It seems that the inherited models from this history of Islam are being adapted for the specific conditions of the modern state. Islamization seems most successful in this particular expression, and calls for more focused study as religious expressions within modern states and societies.

With regard to identity politics and critical activism, moreover, Muslims seem to be engaged in a debate and power struggle over postcolonial

---

Contract in Contemporary Egypt," *International Journal of Middle East Studies* 35, no. 1 (2003): 23–49.

politics in different contexts in Africa. They are sometimes dissatisfied with the distribution of symbols in the state, and sometimes with the values that emerge from ancient texts. The framework of public Islam and Muslim publics provides a lens for examining such discourses. As politics, such discourses should be subjected to more critical and in-depth studies of culture and religion in modern political contexts. Such a politics should be located as part of the history of Islamic politics in the particular region, country, or the history of Islam. Particular attention should be paid to inherited symbols or forms of engagement and disengagement. As these trends are then modified and appropriated for postcolonial contexts, such political discourses (Muslim publics) should also be placed alongside Christian and other cultural expressions and traditions. Together, they should be further developed to enrich political theory in Africa in particular, and political theory in general. The work on identity politics, for example, seems to be preoccupied with Western, liberal democracies. The politics of public Islam should be addressed to this literature. As one of the dominant forms of identity politics in Africa, the politics of public Islam calls for greater comparative and theoretical reflection. This can only happen when the focus on the construction of Islam is replaced with a focus on politics.

There is much more going on within Islamization than politics, however. And this opens up even greater opportunities to examine Muslim publics, again beyond their expressions of Islam. Some of the examples that I have brought up in this paper suggest that Islamization impacts education and the institutionalization of Muslim practices in modern societies. To these can be added developments in health care, marriage relations, consumption patterns, and public preaching. In each case, studies on Muslim publics could be opportunities for sustained and in-depth examinations of social life. As in politics described above, such studies call for greater attention to the impact of religious (Islamic) values and teachings in these spheres of public life (health, marriages, consumption, interfaith relations, and education). As Muslims access texts and ideas from the past, and insert them in creative ways in public life, the rich social and intellectual history of Islam should be included in the analysis. As in politics, new ideas on marital relations, for example, compete and encounter received expectations and role models in historical Muslim societies. And in each case, such studies should be compared with parallel or intersecting developments in Christianity and other religious cultural traditions. And similarly, such studies should then enrich our general understanding of the impact and role of religion in general, and Islam in particular, in public life. The focus would then move from Islam to ethics, values, or forms of engagement.

In conclusion, then, public Islam and Muslim publics provide a useful framework for understanding how technology and new social and political contexts have led to discourses of religion in the public sphere. However, scholarly attention to these public spheres has been guided by the different impacts of Wilfred Cantwell Smith and Jürgen Habermas. Smith's theory of reification has focused attention on the production of Islam(s), while Habermas's work has focused attention on the production of new values for democratic politics. Muslim publics in Africa and elsewhere point to a diversity of engagements that call for more critical reflection and analysis. Apart from a new politics, I have pointed to the role of inherited traditions and values in modern public spheres that call for critical and comparative study.

Works Cited

Abu Zeid, Nasr Hamid. "The Modernisation of Islam or the Islamisation of Modernity." In *Cosmopolitanism, Identity and Authenticity in the Middle East*, edited by Roel Meijer, 71–86. Surrey, Eng.: Curzon, 1999.

Adelkhah, Fariba. "Islam and the Common Mortal." In *Modernizing Islam: Religion in the Public Sphere in the Middle East and Europe*, edited by John Esposito and Francois Burgat, 103–23. London: Hurst, 2003.

Akhavi, Shahrough. "Sunni Modernist Theories of Social Contract in Contemporary Egypt." *International Journal of Middle East Studies* 35, no. 1 (2003): 23–49.

Allievi, Stefano. "Islam in the Public Space: Social Networks, Media and Neo-Communities." In *Muslim Networks and Transnational Communities in and Across Europe*, edited by Stefano Allievi and Jorgen Nielsen, 1–27. Leiden: Brill, 2003.

Allman, Jean Marie. "'Hewers of Wood, Carriers of Water': Islam, Class, and Politics on the Eve of Ghana's Independence." *African Studies Review* 34, no. 2 (1991): 1–26.

Anderson, Jon W. "New Media, New Publics: Reconfiguring the Public Sphere of Islam." *Social Research* 70, no. 3 (2003): 887–906.

Anderson, Jon W., and Yves Gonzales-Quijano. "Technological Mediation and the Emergence of Transnational Muslim Publics." In *Public Islam and the Common Good*, edited by Armando Salvatore and Dale E. Eickelman, 53–71. Leiden: Brill, 2004.

Arabi, Oussama. "The Dawning of the Third Millennium on Shari'a: Egypt's Law No. 1 of 2000, or Women May Divorce at Will." *Arab Law Quarterly* 16, no. 1 (2001): 2–21.

Benhabib, Seyla. *The Claims of Culture: Equality and Diversity in the Global Era*. Princeton, N.J.: Princeton University Press, 2002.

Bowen, John R. "Beyond Migration: Islam as a Transnational Public Space." *Journal of Ethnic and Migration Studies* 30, no. 5 (2003): 879–94.

Brenner, Louis. *Controlling Knowledge: Religion, Power and Schooling in a West African Muslim Society*. London: Hurst, 2000.

Brown, Leon Carl. "The Islamic Reformist Movement in North Africa." *Journal of Modern African Studies* 2, no. 1 (1964): 55–63.

Casanova, José. "Civil Society and Religion: Retrospective Reflections on Catholicism and Prospective Reflections on Islam." *Social Research* 68, no. 4 (2001): 1041–80.

Christelow, Allan. "Ritual, Culture and Politics of Islamic Reformism in Algeria." *Middle Eastern Studies* 23, no. 3 (1987): 255–74.

Constantin, François. "Muslims and Politics: The Attempts to Create Muslim National Organisations in Tanzania, Uganda and Kenya." In *Religion and Politics in East Africa: The Period Since Independence*, edited by Holger Bernt Hansen and Michael Twaddle, 19–31. London: James Curry, 1995.

Didier, Brian J. "When Disputes Turn Public: Heresy, the Common Good, and the State in South India." In *Public Islam and the Common Good*, edited by Armando Salvatore and Dale E. Eickelman, 157–77. Leiden: Brill, 2004.

Dieste, Josep Lluís Mateo. "'Demonstrating Islam': The Conflict of Text and the *Mudawwana* Reform in Morocco." *The Muslim World* 99 (2009): 134–54.

Eickelman, Dale E., and Jon W. Anderson. "Redefining Muslim Publics." In *New Media in the Muslim World: The Emerging Public Sphere*, edited by Dale E. Eickelman and Jon W. Anderson, 1–18. Bloomington: Indiana University Press, 1999.

Esack, Farid. "Three Islamic Strands in the South African Struggle for Justice." *Third World Quarterly* 10, no. 2 (1988): 473–98.

Esposito, John. "Islam and Civil Society." In *Modernizing Islam: Religion in the Public Sphere in the Middle East and Europe*, edited by John Esposito and Francois Burgat, 69–100. London: Hurst, 2003.

Fisher, Humphrey J. "The Juggernaut's Apologia: Conversion to Islam in Black Africa." *Africa: Journal of the International African Institute* 55, no. 2 (1985): 153–73.

Glassman, Jonathan. "Stolen Knowledge: Struggles for Popular Islam on the Swahili Coast, 1870–1963." In *Islam in East Africa: New Sources (Ar-*

chives, Manuscripts and Written Historical Sources: Oral History, Archaeology), edited by Biancamaria Scarcia Amoretti, 209–22. Rome: Herder Editrice le Libreria, 2001.

Gumi, Sheikh Abubakar, and Ismaila Abubakar Tsiga. *Where I Stand?* Ibadan, Nigeria: Spectrum Books, 2001.

Habermas, Jürgen. "On the Relations Between the Secular Liberal State and Religion." In *Political Theologies: Public Religions in a Post-Secular World*, edited by Hent de Vries and Lawrence Sullivan, 251–60. New York: Fordham University Press, 2006.

———. "The Public Sphere: An Encyclopedia Article (1964)." *New German Critique* 3 (1974): 49–55.

Hastings, Adrian. *The Construction of Nationhood: Ethnicity, Religion and Nationalism*. Cambridge, Eng.: Cambridge University Press, 1997.

Haynes, Jeffrey. "Islam and Democracy in East Africa." *Democratization* 13, no. 3 (2006): 490–507.

Hefner, Robert W. "Public Islam and the Problem of Democratization." *Sociology of Religion* 62, no. 4 (2001): 491–514.

Hirschkind, Charles. "Civic Virtue and Religious Reason: An Islamic Counterpublic." *Cultural Anthropology* 16, no. 1 (2001): 3–34.

———. *The Ethical Soundscape: Cassette Sermons and Islamic Counterpublics*. New York: Columbia University Press, 2006.

Hunwick, J. O. "An African Case Study of Political Islam." *Annals of the American Academy of Political and Social Science* 524 (1992): 143–55.

Imam, Ayesha, and Sindi Medar-Gould. 2003. "Please Stop the International Amina Lawal Protest Letter Campaigns." http://www.wluml.org/node/1025.

Ismail, Salwa. "Islamism, Re-Islamization and the Fashioning of Muslim Selves: Refiguring the Public Sphere." *Muslim World Journal of Human Rights* 4, no. 1 (2007): 1–21.

Jack, Homer A. "Malam Aminu Kano: A Profile." *Africa Today* 6, no. 4 (1959): 6–10.

Janson, Marloes. "Roaming About for God's Sake: The Upsurge of the Tabligh Jama'at in the Gambia." *Journal of Religion in Africa* 35, no. 4 (2005): 450–81.

———. "'We Are All the Same, Because We All Worship God': The Controversial Case of a Female Saint in the Gambia." *Africa* 76, no. 4 (2006): 502–25.

Johnston, David L. "Maqāṣid al-Sharīʿa: Epistemology and Hermeneutics of Muslim Theologies of Human Rights." *Die Welt des Islams* 47, no. 2 (2007): 149–87.

Kymlicka, Will. *Multicultural Citizenship: A Liberal Theory of Minority Rights*. Oxford: Clarendon, 1995.

Launay, Robert. "Spirit Media: The Electronic Media and Islam Among Dyula of Northern Cote d'Ivoire." *Africa: Journal of the International African Institute* 67, no. 3 (1997): 441–53.

Lee, Robert D. "Tunisian Intellectuals: Responses to Islamism." *Journal of North African Studies* 13, no. 2 (2008): 157–73.

Lofchie, Michael F. *Zanzibar: Background to Revolution*. Princeton, N.J.: Princeton University Press, 1965.

Loimeier, Roman. "Islamic Reform and Political Change: The Example of Abubakar Gumi and the Yan Izala Movement in Northern Nigeria." In *African Islam and Islam in Africa*, edited by Eva Evers Rosander and David Westerlund, 286–307. London: Hurst, 1997.

———. *Islamic Reform and Political Change in Northern Nigeria*. Series in Islam and Society in Africa. Evanston, Ill.: Northwestern University Press, 1997.

Mahmoud, Mohamed. "Mahmud Muhammad Taha's Second Message of Islam and His Modernist Project." In *Islam and Modernity: Muslim Intellectuals Respond*, edited by John Cooper, Ronald Nettler, and Mohamed Mahmoud, 105–28. London: I. B. Taurus, 2000.

Mazrui, Alamin. "Ethnicity and Pluralism: The Politicization of Religion in Kenya." *Journal of Muslim Minority Affairs* 14, no. 1 (1993): 191–201.

Moosa, Ebrahim. "Prospects of Muslim Law in South Africa: A History and Recent Developments." In *Yearbook of Islamic and Middle Eastern Law, Volume 3*, edited by Eugene Cotran and Chibli Mallat, 130–55. London: Kluwer Law International, 1996.

———. "Worlds 'Apart': Tablighi Jama'at in South Africa Under Apartheid, 1963–1993." *Journal for Islamic Studies* 17 (1997): 28–48.

Na'im, Abdullah Ahmed al-. *Toward an Islamic Reformation: Civil Liberties, Human Rights, and International Law*. Foreword by John Obert Voll. Contemporary Issues in the Middle East. Syracuse, N.Y.: Syracuse University Press, 1990.

Oded, Arye. *Islam and Politics in Kenya*. London: Lynne Rienner, 2000.

Reetz, Dietrich. "The Tablīghī Madrassas in Lenasia and Azaadville: Local Players in the Global 'Islamic Field.'" In *Muslim Schools and Education in South Africa and Europe*, edited by Abdulkader I. Tayob, Inga Niehaus, and Wolfram Weisse, 85–104. Münster: Waxmann Verlag, 2011.

Reichmuth, Stefan. "Education and the Growth of Religious Associations

Among Yoruba Muslims—the Ansaar-ul-Deen Society on Nigeria." *Journal of Religion in Africa* 26, no. 4 (1996): 365–405.

———. "New Trends in Islamic Education in Nigeria: A Preliminary Account." *Die Welt des Islams, New Series* 29, no. 1/4 (1989): 41–60.

———. "A Regional Centre of Islamic Learning in Nigeria: Ilorin and Its Influence on Yoruba Islam." In *Madrasa: La transmission du savoir dans le monde musulman*, edited by Nicole Grandin and Marc Gaborieu, 229–45. Paris: XP Editions Arguments, 1997.

Rosander, Eva Evers. "Introduction: The Islamization of 'Tradition' and 'Modernity.'" In *African Islam and Islam in Africa: Encounters Between Sufis and Islamists*, edited by David Westerlund and Eva Evers Rosander, 1–27. London: Hurst and Company in cooperation with the Nordic Africa Institute, Uppsala, Sweden, 1997.

Salvatore, Armando. *Islam and the Political Discourse of Modernity*. Vol. 4, International Politics of the Middle East. Reading, Eng.: Ithaca, 1997.

Salvatore, Armando, and Dale E. Eickelman. "Muslim Publics." In *Public Islam and the Common Good*, edited by Armando Salvatore and Dale E. Eickelman, 3–27. Leiden: Brill, 2004.

———. "Preface: Public Islam and the Common Good." In *Public Islam and the Common Good*, edited by Armando Salvatore and Dale E. Eickelman, xi–xxv. Leiden: Brill, 2004.

———, eds. *Public Islam and the Common Good*. Social, Economic, and Political Studies of the Middle East and Asia 95. Leiden: Brill, 2004.

———. "The Public Sphere and Muslim Identities." *European Journal of Sociology* 43 (2002): 92–115.

Sanneh, Lamin. "Translatability in Islam and in Christianity in Africa: A Thematic Approach." In *Religion in Africa: Experience and Expression*, edited by Thomas D. Blakely, Walter E. A. van Beek, and Dennis L. Thomson, 22–45. London: James Curry, 1994.

Sayed, Muhammad Khalid. "The Shifting World of South African Madrasahs, 1973–2008." M.A. thesis. University of Cape Town, 2010.

Schulz, Dorothea E. "'Charisma and Brotherhood' Revisited: Mass-Mediated Forms of Spirituality in Urban Mali." *Journal of Religion in Africa: Religion and the Media* 33, no. 2 (2003): 146–71.

Scott, Joan W. "Multiculturalism and the Politics of Identity." In *The Identity in Question*, edited by John Rajchman, 3–12. New York: Routledge, 1995.

Seeseman, Rüdiger. "African Islam or Islam in Africa? Evidence from Kenya." In *The Global Worlds of the Swahili: Interfaces of Islam, Identity and Space in 19th and 20th-Century East Africa*, edited by Rüdiger Seeseman and Roman Loimeier, 229–50. Berlin: Lit Verlag, 2006.

Shahin, Emad Eldin. *Political Ascent: Contemporary Islamic Movements in North Africa*. Boulder, Colo.: Westview, 1997.

Smith, Wilfred Cantwell. *The Meaning and End of Religion*. San Francisco: Harper and Row, 1978.

Soares, Benjamin F. *Islam and the Prayer Economy: History and Authority in a Malian Town*. Edinburgh, Ann Arbor: Edinburgh University Press; University of Michigan Press for the International African Institute, 2005.

Starret, Gregory. *Putting Islam to Work: Education, Politics, and Religious Transformation in Egypt*. Berkeley: University of California Press, 1998.

Taylor, Charles. *Multiculturalism and "the Politics of Recognition": An Essay by Charles Taylor with Commentary by Amy Gutmann, Steven C. Rockefeller, Michael Walzer, Susan Wolf*. Edited by Amy Gutmann. Princeton, N.J.: Princeton University Press, 1992.

Tayob, Abdulkader. *Islam in South Africa: Mosques, Imams and Sermons*. Gainesville: University of South Florida Press, 1999.

———, ed. *Muslim Marriages in South Africa: From Constitution to Legislation: Papers Presented at Muslim Marriages Workshop, Saturday 22 May 2010, Capetonian Hotel*. Cape Town: Centre for Contemporary Islam, University of Cape Town, 2011.

———. "Race, Ideology, and Islam in Contemporary South Africa." In *Islam in World Cultures: Comparative Perspectives*, edited by R. Michael Feener, 253–82. Santa Barbara, Calif.: ABC CLIO, 2004.

Tayob, Abdulkader, Inga Niehaus, and Wolfram Weisse, eds. *Muslim Schools and Education in South Africa and Europe*. Religionen im Dialog. Münster: Waxmann, 2011.

Turner, Simon. "'These Young Men Show No Respect for Local Customs'—Globalization and Islamic Revival in Zanzibar." *Journal of Religion in Africa* 39, no. 3 (2009): 237–61.

Vahed, Goolam. "Contesting 'Orthodoxy': The Tablighi-Sunni Conflict Among South African Muslims in the 1970s and 1980s." *Journal of Muslim Minority Affairs* 23, no. 2 (2003): 313–34.

Remembrance of Muhammad Idris Muhammad Saleh (Maalim Idris), 1934–2012

*Anne Bang,** CHR. MICHELSEN INSTITUTE, NORWAY

DOI: 10.5192/215409930302169

Muhammad Idris Muhammad Saleh died in Zanzibar on March 5, 2012, aged 78. Known locally as Maalim Idris (or Maalim Idrisa), his impact on the Zanzibari community was first and foremost as a religious leader and a teacher, but also as a keeper of the history of Islamic scholarship in East Africa, a writer, and a collector.

Maalim Idris was born into a Comorian family in Zanzibar, the oldest of eight siblings. The Comorians as a group were well represented among the educated classes both in Bū Saʿīdī times and in the colonial era, and the family of Maalim Idris was no exception. His father was a teacher and a schoolmaster, and Maalim Idris followed the same path after first receiving both a secular and a religious education. In 1950 he enrolled at the Zanzibar Teacher Training College, and immediately after graduation he started teaching in the government school in Dole, north of Zanzibar town. In the next three decades he taught in several different schools on Unguja, while also working as a madrasa teacher.

Following his retirement from government service in the 1980s, Maalim Idris took a more active role in the Rahma Mosque in the Shangani quarter of Stone town. In 1985 he became imam there. He was also

* This remembrance originally appeared on the East Africa blog, edited by Shamil Jeppie of University of Cape Town. The text is available in English and French at http://www.tombouctoumanuscripts.org/blog.

Islamic Africa, VOL. 3, NO. 2, 2012. ISSN 2154-0993. www.islamicafricajournal.org

instrumental in developing the madrasa of that mosque, drawing children and youngsters from the neighborhood and beyond. Maalim's concern for the next generation and for education also ran deep in his work in the madrasa, and he was known to introduce unconventional subjects on occasion. In the 1990s, he hired a French tutor who taught French after regular madrasa classes. In the past decade, he also introduced computer classes for boys and girls in the madrasa, and installed a computer room on the second floor.

In line with his educational zeal, Maalim Idris founded the nongovernmental organization (NGO) "Islamic Madrasa Relief Organization" in the 1990s. This organization offered financial assistance to orphans to pay for madrasa education, organized youth activities, and funded religious teachers in poorer areas of Zanzibar. In recent years, the organization also provided food to children of poorer families who were hard hit by rising food prices. Another example of his community involvement—and his lifelong attachment to his Comorian roots—was his role in the Mwinye Baraka Foundation, which is a charitable organization named after the Comorian Islamic scholar Mwinye Baraka (Sayyid Umar Abdallah, 1917–1988).

Maalim Idris was an involved community member and served on several local committees and groups, including *mawlid* committees and a neighborhood committee for the Shangani quarter, known to voice opinions on everything from the impact of mass tourism to parking regulations. He was a member of the "Baraza of Elders" in the Ukutani quarter. From 2006 he was a member of the executive committee of the Zanzibar Outreach Programme, an NGO that—among other activities—promotes education for the deaf and community clinics in remote areas.

From the point of view of Islamic history, Maalim Idris's greatest impact was undoubtedly as a collector of items pertaining to the Zanzibar and East African past. His growing, and eventually substantial, collection, combined with his willingness to share material with all those interested in the subject, made his apartment a well-known center for local and foreign academics alike. I was fortunate enough to be one of them. Research periods in Zanzibar always included the "morning reports" in Maalim Idris's apartment, with coffee and discussions over anything from the endless twists of Zanzibar politics to international events, and the price of rice and gasoline to East African Islamic history. Occasionally, I would revisit a question from the day before, and Maalim would get up and say "Yes, about that; I found something . . ." and hand me a document that I had thought unobtainable—clearly from somewhere in the deep corners of his collection.

To the historian, the manuscripts, books, and other textual materials that were in his possession are obviously valuable as historical sources. This is particularly so in a society that, due to the 1964 revolution and the exodus of many of the scholarly families from the islands, has much less textual material than could be expected given the history of Zanzibar as a scholarly center. For example, the Sumayṭ family left in 1965, taking with them the entire library of the father and son Ahmad and Umar b. Sumayṭ, both of them former chief *qadis* and prominent Muslim scholars. Other libraries went to Europe or the Persian Gulf, either with the families that left, or later, by other means. In some cases, manuscripts were simply buried or burned.

Among the most important items in Maalim Idris's collection are approximately thirty manuscripts dating from 1860 to 1910. These are both Ibāḍī and Shāfiʿī and contain poetry, *mawlids,* legal material, grammatical works, medicine, and (at least) two Qur'ans, all of them in Arabic. Some are locally authored, others are locally produced copies of standard works, while others, in turn, were imported from the Middle East during the late nineteenth century. The manuscripts come from different collections, but some of them must, by internal evidence, have belonged to the Zanzibari-Comorian scholar and teacher Burhān Mkelle (1884–1949). In addition, the collection contain several more recent manuscripts, in both Swahili (including *ajami* Swahili) and Arabic, testimony to the continued Islamic scholarly tradition in Zanzibar in the first half of the twentieth century. Finally, the collection also contains an unknown number of books, again previously the property of famous Islamic scholars like Burhan Mkelle and Said b. Dahman (1877–1926), with their personal inscriptions, notes, and *waqfiyyas.* Finally, among the sources pertaining to Islamic scholars can also be found letters, leaflets, prints, and newspaper clippings that are time-consuming—and in some cases impossible—to locate elsewhere. It is the totality, and not only the oldest and most spectacular manuscripts, that makes this collection an important one for scholars of Islam in East Africa. In the past decade, several works have been published by East African, Japanese, and European researchers that refer to material in Maalim Idris's collection, my own works included.

However, Maalim Idris himself saw the collection not merely as a source for academic books and dissertations. As he pointed out, what was left of Islamic manuscripts in Zanzibar has either been deposited in the

Zanzibar National Archives or remain in unknown private hands, neither of which ensures immediate accessibility, especially for non-specialists. Showing his true educationalist colors, Maalim Idris used to say that he had collected the material "for the young people," for them to be able to access their history, with a clear reference to a chain of knowledge transmission that was broken during the 1960s and 1970s. His view was that the young generation of Zanzibaris should know the full extent of their history, including the Islamic aspect that, in his view, had been partly eradicated.

Now, when Maalim Idris is no longer with us, we can only hope that his dream will be realized and that the tradition which he spent the better part of his life collecting will be incorporated into the wider, multi-stranded remains of the Zanzibari past and made available to all.

ARTICLES

Urdu as an African Language: A Survey of a Source Literature

*Nile Green,** UCLA

DOI: 10.5192/215409930302173

ABSTRACT

This article provides the first survey of the development of Urdu literature in Africa, with a particular emphasis on East and South Africa. Dealing with the colonial and postcolonial periods, the survey encompasses the early evolution of Indian settler descriptions of Africa before moving on to the range of other genres of African Urdu, including travel writing, hagiography, poetry, and historiography. While in many cases these sources display Islamic cultural and religious concerns, other texts were written by non-Muslim settlers from Punjab. The emergence of these source materials is placed in its historical contexts, particularly colonial South Asian labor and merchant migration and settlement in Africa. Where possible, the Urdu sources are compared to sources in Gujarati and other regional languages.

At the present day large numbers of Indian emigrants are passing over to Natal and other African colonies, and it will be interesting to see what linguistic consequences will ensue.
—"The Urdu Tongue," *The Literary World* (August 30, 1895)

* I am grateful to Ned Alpers, Clare Anderson, Christopher Ehret, Brannon Ingram, Jonathan Miran, Scott Reese, Julia Verne, and the anonymous readers for their helpful suggestions.

Islamic Africa, VOL. 3, NO. 2, 2012. ISSN 2154-0993.

From Indian Settlers to Urdu Sources

In recent years, the Indian Ocean turn in African history has brought increased recognition of the importance of interregional and "oceanic" languages for the study of African history.[1] Portuguese, Dutch, and English sources have long been used to tie East and South African history into larger oceanic and colonial geographies. Among non-European languages, it is naturally Arabic that has dominated the scholarship, with more recent work focusing on the circulation of Arabic and to a lesser extent Swahili texts and their writers into and out of Africa, as well as between different regions of the continent.[2] However, despite decades of scholarly interest in South Asian settlement in Africa, work is only now beginning to make use of source materials in languages from South Asia. Since the nineteenth and early twentieth centuries saw the arrival in Africa of merchants and laborers from various regions of the subcontinent, it seems feasible that materials may at some point be uncovered in such languages as Sindhi, Tamil, or Punjabi. However, at the moment, it is scholarship on Gujarati that has led the way. Working with the translators Vimla Chavda and Sharrifa Keshavjee, Cynthia Salvadori and Julia Aldrick have brought to light the important 1902 Gujarati travelogue of Ebrahimji Noorbhai Adamji, which recounts a merchant expedition along the tracks of the expanding Uganda Railway.[3] Savita Nair's study of South Asian migration to East Africa has also uncovered a series of Gujarati epistolary sources, including

---

[1] R. Loimeier and R. Seesemann, eds., *The Global Worlds of the Swahili: Interfaces of Islam, Identity and Space in 19th and 20th-Century East Africa* (Berlin: Lit, 2006); J. Miran, *Red Sea Citizens: Cosmopolitan Society and Cultural Change in Massawa* (Bloomington: Indiana University Press, 2009); and S. S. Reese, *Renewers of the Age: Holy Men and Social Discourse in Colonial Benaadir* (Leiden: Brill, 2008).

[2] On Arabic, see A. K. Bang, *Sufis and Scholars of the Sea: Family Networks in East Africa, 1860–1925* (London: RoutledgeCurzon, 2003); and S. S. Reese, "The Adventures of Abu Harith: Muslim Travel Writing and Navigating the Modern in Colonial East Africa," in *The Transmission of Learning in Islamic Africa,* ed. S. S. Reese (Leiden: Brill, 2004). On Swahili, see Abdallah Salih Farsy, *The Shafi'i Ulama of East Africa, c. 1830–1970: A Hagiographic Account,* trans. and ed. R. L. Pouwels (Madison: African Studies Program, University of Wisconsin-Madison, 1989), the biographies in which outline a pattern of increasing Middle Eastern travels by East African 'ulama during the late nineteenth and early twentieth centuries.

[3] C. Salvadori, ed., *Two Indian Travellers: East Africa, 1902–1905* (Mombasa: Friends of Fort Jesus, 1997).

Narasimbhai Ishwarbhai Patel's printed *Africa na Pathro* (*Letters from Africa*, published 1932).[4] Tracing the "return" of Afro-Indian Sidis to East Africa, Helen Basu has studied a post-colonial Gujarati travelogue from 1972.[5] While these pioneering works are important, at present this Gujarati corpus still constitutes a very small number of texts, albeit with more presumably waiting to be discovered. Gujarati was after all the main language used between members of the Afro-Indian Gujarati trading network that grew significantly from the mid-nineteenth century. However, even within South Asia, Gujarati remained either a regional or a community language and never found the broader geographical and social reach of such languages as Persian and Urdu.

Building on the findings of scholars working with Gujarati materials and my own earlier work on Urdu in South Africa, the aim of this article is to introduce Urdu to the larger field of African studies.[6] For while never recognized as a source language for African history, from at least the first decade of the twentieth century (and quite possibly beforehand) there emerged a significant body of materials in Urdu on the South Asian presence in Africa. As the outline in the following pages hopes to demonstrate, these materials afford unique "insider" insight into the cultural, religious, and intellectual dimensions of South Asian (and particularly South Asian Muslim) interactions with Africa and its peoples that no amount of colonial archival material in English can hope to capture. The opportunity here is greater than tracking down materials on "Indians in Africa." For the following pages propose that with a written textual presence in Africa that dates back to at least 1900, Urdu should be seen as an African language in its own right, albeit based on a model of African written languages being more typically interregional than national in their range. By framing Urdu as an African language that is nonetheless an oceanic and interregional Islamic language like Arabic, we may help re-conceptualize older area studies approaches to the history of East and South Africa in a way that recent

[4] S. Nair, "Moving Life Histories: Gujarat, East Africa and the Indian Diaspora, 1880–2000" (Ph.D. dissertation, University of Pennsylvania, 2001).

[5] H. Basu, "Politics of Travelling in the Postcolonial Indian Ocean World: Sidi Abdula bin Mubarak's *My Journey to East Africa*," *Ziff Journal* 2 (2005).

[6] On Urdu in South Africa, see N. S. Green, *Bombay Islam: The Religious Economy of the West Indian Ocean, 1840–1915* (New York: Cambridge University Press, 2011); and N. S. Green, "The Dilemmas of the Pious Biographer: Missionary Islam and the Oceanic Hagiography," *Journal of Religious History* 34, no. 4 (2010).

work has done with regard to the South Asian presence in Arabia or the African and Middle Eastern presence in India.[7]

The first step with regard to Urdu is to unhitch the language from South Asian geographies and nationalisms. For if Urdu has usually seen its history framed in a bounded subcontinental geography, and served (albeit more ideologically than practically) as a national language for Pakistan, then the fuller contours of its actual usage spread way beyond the political and spatial limits of South Asia. For despite the usage of Urdu (or more properly, "Dakani" and "Rekhta") as a poetic language in early modern (and in a few instances, medieval) South Asia, Urdu evolved as a prose literature in the colonial age of steam and print. As a result, in the later nineteenth and twentieth centuries Urdu was read and written wherever South Asian Urdu-users (both Muslim and non-Muslim) traveled and settled. While almost entirely ignored by the scholarship, by the first decade of the twentieth century Urdu works were being written and even published in such disparate cities as London, Aden, Cairo, and Istanbul.[8] Such texts map a process of linguistic trans-regionalization (even globalization) that not only saw Muslims from different linguistic regions of India choosing to learn Urdu, but also saw the language expanding through the steamship networks of the period. South Asians residing overseas came to sufficiently identify with the language as to create new Urdu enclaves in Durban and Mombasa where, as we see below, Urdu language classes, journals, and poetry circles were gradually established in the early twentieth century.[9]

Before turning to some brief sample studies of specific textual examples, it is worth developing this sense of Urdu as an "Islamic language" somewhat further and then qualifying it.[10] Muslim writers of Urdu often consciously drew on (and in many cases still read) Arabic and Persian works. Muslim Urdu writings, then, were in many cases deliberately positioned in relation to this older Perso-Arabic ecumene through the adoption of the

---

[7] Green, *Bombay Islam;* and J. M. Willis, "Making Yemen Indian: Rewriting the Boundaries of Imperial Arabia," *International Journal of Middle East Studies* 41, no. 1 (2009).

[8] On Urdu in Cairo, see Jalāl al-Hafnāwī, "'Islāmī Dunyā' Misr sē Shā'i' Shoda Urdū kā Akhbār," *Khuda Bakhsh Library Journal* 110 (1994).

[9] On Urdu usage in Mombasa and Nairobi, see W. H. Whiteley, *Language in Kenya* (Nairobi: Oxford University Press, 1974), 71, 275, 305.

[10] T. Rahman, "Urdu as an Islamic Language," *Annual of Urdu Studies* 21 (2006); and C. Shackle, "Urdu Poetry as a Vehicle for Islamic Re-Expression," in *Religious Perspectives in Modern Muslim and Jewish Literatures*, ed. H. Kilpatrick and G. Abramson (London: Routledge, 2006).

genres, conceptual vocabulary, or other conventions of this earlier literature. Urdu's arrival in Africa was therefore not the sudden intervention of a new language, but instead part of a longer process of the circulation of trans-regional written languages around the Indian Ocean. If Urdu can certainly not claim the level of interethnic participation achieved over a much longer period by Arabic, then it is nonetheless important to stress the variety of Urdu's users. For if these users were mainly of South Asian origin, within that broad category were included people of a range of ethnicities and religions; people who used Urdu as either a first or a second language; and people who were born and lived as far apart as Bombay, Lahore, Cairo, London, or Durban. This broad user base included various non-Muslim groups including Hindus and Sikhs, in particular communities that had migrated from colonial Punjab where Urdu had formed the standard language of education in government schools. If not on the scale achieved by Arabic (or English), Urdu did serve as a trans-regional lingua franca around the Indian Ocean. And for its Muslim users, it served to connect them to the older literary traditions of Arabic and Persian that had spread through the region in previous centuries.

Contexts of a New African Literature

As it did in the Atlantic at the same time, the arrival of the steam age represented the great moment of transformation in the cities of the Indian Ocean, a transformation signaled first by the regular relay of steamships between African and South Asian ports and second by the transformation of those ports into railheads with the appearance of railroads on either side of the ocean, from Bombay in 1853, Suez in 1858, Durban in 1860, and Mombasa in 1896. These transformations were social and cultural no less than technological. Cheap steam travel enabled migration on a far larger scale than the previous centuries of Afro-Indian contact, lowering access to travel down the social ladder to indentured laborers and entrepreneurial middle-class "passenger Indians" in a process that by the time of the opening of East Africa in the 1890s had already been underway farther south in Natal for some three decades.[11] In the half century from 1860 to 1911,

[11] On South Asian settlement in South Africa, see S. Bhana and J. Brain, *Setting Down Roots: Indian Migrants in South Africa, 1860–1911* (Johannesburg: Witwatersrand University Press, 1990); and P. Gervais-Lambony, F. Landy, and S. Oldfield, eds., *Reconfiguring Identities and Building Territories in India and South Africa* (Delhi: Manohar, 2005).

over 150,000 South Asian laborers migrated to Natal, many of whom were familiar with Urdu from their homelands in the "Hindi/Urdu belt" of the United Provinces.[12] Turning from South to East Africa, in just the few years between 1896 and 1902, almost 32,000 South Asian laborers arrived in Mombasa on steamships from Bombay and Karachi, the majority from Punjab where Urdu was a language of vernacular education.[13] While many returned to India, those who stayed on added a new social profile to the older and smaller community of South Asian (and largely Gujarati) merchants.

These mass labor migrations had been preceded by the expansion of a smaller and much wealthier merchant diaspora whose presence in East Africa reached back to at least the sixteenth century. With the growth of such trading ports as Mogadishu and Zanzibar in the middle years of the nineteenth century, South Asian merchants became more important commercial players than ever and as a result began to settle in larger numbers, establishing merchant houses with increasingly regularly connected outposts in such ports as Bombay and to a lesser extent Karachi as well as their smaller African counterparts. Attracted by the visible profits being made by these British Indian subjects, India-based imperialists promoted the expansion of British commercial and eventually political expansion along the East African coastline as the Imperial British East Africa Company (founded 1888) briefly flourished before ceding administration of British East Africa and Uganda to the Foreign Office in 1895 and 1896 respectively. As the Omani Empire that had originally enticed South Asian merchants to Zanzibar contracted in the face of German and British expansion, the same merchant houses began to relocate to such emergent imperial port cities as Mombasa. Crucial to South Asian commercial interests no less than British political interests was the Scottish shipping magnate William Mackinnon (1823–1893), the key figure behind the formation of both the Imperial British East Africa Company and the British India Steam Navigation Company, which from the early 1870s connected Zanzibar and then Mombasa to the expanding steam networks of the Indian Ocean and beyond.[14]

---

[12] For statistics, see R. Ebr.-Vally, "Migration of an Identity: South Africans of Indian Descent," in Gervais-Lambony et al., *Reconfiguring Identities,* 224.

[13] For statistics, see T. R. Metcalf, *Imperial Connections: India in the Indian Ocean Arena, 1860–1920* (Berkeley: University of California Press, 2007), 200, citing the *Final Report of the Uganda Railway Committee.*

[14] John S. Galbraith, *Mackinnon and East Africa 1878–1895: A Study in the "New Imperialism"* (Cambridge, Eng.: Cambridge University Press, 1972).

Before turning to the brief sample studies that make up the main body of this article, it is worth addressing the question of why of all South Asian languages Urdu should have played so important a role as a discursive filter of the South Asian experience of Africa? The answer to this question is partly found in the blend of broad intelligibility and prestige that Urdu acquired in the nineteenth century, partly in the profile of South Asian emigration to East Africa, and partly in the massive expansion of Urdu printing during the period. If Urdu has often been notionally connected to an inland Urdu "heartland" along the Ganges plain of northern India, then this geographical characterization belies the fact that during the nineteenth century Urdu also became a major lingua franca of Bombay and from there of the western Indian Ocean trading stations as a whole, including those in East Africa. By the 1890s, "Hindustani" Urdu was being described as "being spoken by very many Somalis [and] is practically the official language of the country," while in Zanzibar even Sultan Sayyid bin Sultan was said to have been conversant in Hindustani.[15] Powered in part by trade and print, this interregional reach connected readers and listeners in various regions of India as well as overseas and set Urdu apart from other more determinedly regional languages such as Gujarati or Punjabi, which were only spoken within the bounds of specific communities.

As we have noted, the language's appearance in Africa must also be partly explained in connection with the profile of South Asian emigration to South and East Africa. Urdu was to develop close connections with both regions, though the position of Urdu must always be seen in relation to other languages spoken or written among South Asians in Africa, such as Gujarati and Tamil. However, what distinguished Urdu from such regional and community languages was its role as a trans-regional lingua franca among not only Muslims from different areas of the subcontinent, but also among Hindus and Sikhs exposed to Urdu through their origins in the Urdu heartlands of the United Provinces or Punjab, where Urdu was an official language of education. While a large proportion of the indentured labor force that migrated to South Africa originated in the United Provinces (as well as Tamil Nadu), in East Africa the demographic profile of migration was even more positively inclined toward Urdu due to the fact that the majority of the Uganda Railway labor migrants came from Punjab and

[15] M. R. Bhacker, *Trade and Empire in Muscat and Zanzibar: Roots of British Domination* (London: Routledge, 1994), 69; and M. McNeill, *In Pursuit of the "Mad" Mullah: Service and Sport in the Somali Protectorate* (London: C.A. Pearson, 1902), 274.

other regions adjacent to Karachi.[16] While not necessarily mother-tongue speakers of Urdu, many of these Punjabis were deeply familiar with Urdu as a result of the colonial implementation of Urdu as Punjab's official language of government and education after the region's annexation by the East India Company in 1849. The presence of many Muslims among the railway workers added a religious layer to the language's exportation, since by the late nineteenth century some degree of educated exposure to Urdu was widespread among almost all Punjabi Muslims. Moreover, the profile of labor migrants who sailed to Mombasa was more professionally diverse than those who migrated to work on the plantations of Natal, since the building of the Uganda Railway and the management of its vast workforce required educated South Asian technicians and accountants who were necessarily literate, with "Hindustani" Urdu in addition forming the most widespread common language between South Asian employees and their British overseers. Punjabi Muslims came to have an especially close relationship with Urdu: it was from Sialkot in the heart of Punjab that there emerged the greatest of all modern Urdu poets, Muhammad Iqbal (1877–1938), while by 1900 the Punjabi city of Lahore was one of the most important Urdu publishing centers in the whole of India.[17] The Punjabi profile of South Asian migration to East Africa therefore rendered Urdu a natural literary outlet in terms of both reading and writing. In dealings with the South Asian traders who followed the laying of the train line into the interior, spoken "Hindustani" Urdu again served as the most efficient South Asian lingua franca, especially since even Gujarati merchants connected with Bombay already used it as a spoken business language.

This perspective is echoed in the various accounts written in Urdu itself of the development of the language and of East Africa's South Asian communities more generally. In his *Bahar-e Urdu Gulshan-e Mashriqi Afriqa Men* (*Urdu Springtime in the Rose Garden of East Africa*), Kalidas Gupta Riza (1925–2001) dates the importing of Urdu to East Africa as

[16] On Punjabi dominance among the Uganda Railway immigrants, see P. G. Forster, M. Hitchcock, and F. F. Lyimo, *Race and Ethnicity in East Africa* (New York: St. Martin's, 2000), 83; and M. Mann, "'*How Many People Were Crying Oceans': Südasiatische Migranten im Indischen Ozean,*" in *Der Indische Ozean: Das afro-asiatische Mittelmeer als Kultur- und Wirtschaftsraum,* ed. D. Rothermund and S. Weigelin-Schwiedrzik (Vienna: Promedia, 2004), 136.

[17] On the increasing importance of Punjab-based writers for Urdu, see F. Mir, *The Social Space of Language: Vernacular Culture in British Colonial Punjab* (Berkeley: University of California Press, 2010).

coinciding with the arrival of the first Uganda Railway workers in 1896.[18] Seeking to maintain memories of their homeland, Punjabi railway workers relied on Urdu, which was for Punjabis of various religious backgrounds the main language of reading and writing and remained so for those who chose to settle in Africa.[19] Even when the Hindu reformist association Arya Samaj arrived in British East Africa in 1899 (and in South Africa in 1908), it turned to Urdu for its outreach into the South Asian community, using the spoken language in its Vedic Church (1899) and Samaj Mandir temple (1908), as well as in its printed literature in East Africa.[20] Kalidas Gupta Riza also notes how Urdu benefited from the series of libraries that from the 1900s and 1910s began to be established in Mombasa and subsequently in other towns connected by the railway. These included the Seif bin Salim Library founded in Mombasa in 1903 (which was almost exclusively devoted to Indian books) and such other libraries as the Railway Indian Institute Library, the Kokani Muslim Free Library, the Desai Memorial Library, the Sanatan Dharm Sabha Library, and the Arya Samaj Library.[21] While in many cases, Urdu books written either in or for Africa were printed in South Asian cities such as Bombay, Lahore, and Karachi, this was more a reflection of the economics of publishing than of the language's fixed place of "belonging." After all, the period also saw South Asian companies printing Swahili and Arabic books for the African marketplace.[22] As printed commodities no less than source texts, Urdu writings were part of an oceanic literary marketplace that was fueled by the interaction of supply and demand on both sides of the Indian Ocean.[23]

The following sections now turn to a sample series of genres in which Urdu texts written in and about Africa are available. While the selection

[18] Kālīdās Guptā Rizā, *Bahār-e Urdū Gulshan-e Mashriqī Afrīqa Men* (Bombay: Mawdrān, 1992), 33–36.

[19] Ibid., 34.

[20] Ibid., 35–36. On the Arya Samaj in Punjab and South Africa, see I. Bannga, "Arya Samaj and Punjabi Identity," in *Punjabi Identity in a Global Context,* ed. P. Singh and S. Singh Thandi (Delhi: Oxford University Press, 1999); and T. Naidoo, *The Arya Samaj Movement in South Africa* (Delhi: Motilal Banarsidass, 1992).

[21] Kālīdās Guptā Rizā, *Bahār-e Urdū,* 36. More generally, see A.-B. Wallenius, *Libraries in East Africa* (Uppsala: Nordic Africa Institute, 1971). On awareness in South Asia of conditions in East Africa through letters and newspaper reports, see Nair, "Moving Life Histories," chapter 3.

[22] On such printed book exports, see Green, *Bombay Islam,* 95–99.

[23] Ibid.

of genres is not meant to be exhaustive, it does point out what appear to be the major types of text to have been written. This weighting of genres appears to reflect not only the prominence of certain genres (such as the *ghazal* poem) within the Urdu canon more generally, but also the specific historical conditions of Urdu's expansion into Africa. In reflection of the latter, the first of these genres to which we will turn is the travelogue.

The Travelogue

Although after the emergence of the first literary clubs in the region it would be in terms of poetry and community histories that the greater part of East African Urdu writing would be written, the earliest major Urdu account of East Africa written in the region itself belonged to the genre of the *safarnama* or "travelogue." Written in 1901 and published in 1904, perhaps the earliest Urdu book on East Africa is the *Safarnama-e Uganda wa Mumbasa* (henceforth *Safarnama-e Uganda*).[24] This was by no means the earliest African travelogue to be published in Urdu, for an Urdu edition of Mungo Park's *Travels in the Interior Districts of Africa* had been printed in Calcutta as early as 1853.[25] Many more Urdu travelogues dealing with West as well as East and South Africa would later be written from the mid-twentieth century. However, as the earliest currently known Urdu account of an Indian journey in Africa, it is toward the *Safarnama-e Uganda* and the travelogue genre to which it belonged that we now turn for the first sample study.

As a genre, the Urdu travelogue emerged as the younger sibling of the Arabic *rihla* travelogue, both of which had pre-industrial antecedents before expanding tremendously with the cheaper availability of travel in the age of the steamship. The counterparts to the Urdu travelogue discussed here were such Arabic texts as the *rihla* of Abu Harith, which outlined a sequence of early twentieth-century travels undertaken from Zanzibar.[26] The Urdu travelogue itself was characterized by a blend of the literary and

---

[24] Anonymous, *Safarnāma-e Ūgandā wa Mumbāsā* (Lahore: Khādim al-Ta'līm Istīm Prēs, 1904), henceforth *Safarnāma* (1904). For a fuller study of this text, see N. S. Green, "Africa in Indian Ink: Urdu Articulations of Indian Settlement in East Africa," *Journal of African History* 53, no. 2 (2012).

[25] Mungō Pārk [Mungo Park (1771–1806)], *Safarnāma Mungō Pārk Sāhib Kā* (Calcutta, 1853).

[26] Reese, "Adventures of Abu Harith."

informational through the legacy of its twin origins in the polished Persian travelogues of previous centuries that were its generic ancestors and the more robustly practical ethos of the Victorian age of its own emergence.[27] While the most famous Urdu travelogues concerned voyages to the imperial center in Britain, other texts presented information on the new imperial regions of Burma and East Africa that saw South Asian settlement.[28] In such cases, the travelogues served quite practical purposes of purveying information about climate, culture, and living conditions for potential but undecided migrants back home.

The *Safarnama-e Uganda* was printed in Lahore as a lithograph in 1904 on a steam press belonging to the al-Ta'lim ("Education") publishing house.[29] The name of the author does not appear in the text, and the title page featured only the name of the publisher, Munshi Muhammad 'Abd al-'Aziz. However, certain clues throughout the text allow us to make certain assumptions about the author. In a preface written in the stylized form of a final testament containing "guidance" (*nasihat*) to his son, the author dated the completion of the text to May 31, 1901, adding several pages later that it was in June 1900 that he set off on his journey from Punjab to East Africa.[30] In the preface the author also named his son as Muzaffar al-Din, adding several pages later that his friend (and fellow traveler?) Munshi Karim Bakhsh of Jalandhar helped him complete the text.[31] With their expressions of regret at missing loved ones and words of final advice to a son the author felt he would not see grow into manhood, the tone of the preface and formal foreword (*dibacha*) suggest that the author was dying or at least suffering from a grave illness when he wrote this final section of the text, presumably before entrusting it to Munshi Karim Bakhsh for completion. Finally, the extensive details that the travelogue provided on the Uganda Railway—indeed, the text's geographical vision of East Africa is entirely based around the railway—strongly suggests that its anonymous author was one of the thousands of Punjabi migrants from this period who worked on the railway. Along with mention of his dear friend Munshi

[27] On the earlier history of the Urdu travelogue, see Wahīd Qurēshī, *Urdū Adab men Safarnāma* (Lahore: Qawmī Prēs, n.d.), part 3.

[28] Mawlwī 'Abd al-Khalīq Khān, *Sayr-e Barhmā* (Lucknow: Matba'a Mīnā Lakhnaw, 1310/1893).

[29] For a fuller study of the text, see Green, "Africa in Indian Ink."

[30] *Safarnāma (1904),* 3, 4.

[31] *Safarnāma (1904),* 1, 5.

(that is, "secretary" or "clerk") Karim Bakhsh, the author's level of education (apparent not only in the formal literary qualities of the text but also in his reference to Arabic books he had read) suggests that he was likewise one of the many educated secretaries or *munshis* who accompanied the South Asian laborers to oversee the lower-level bureaucratic aspects of the project and act as intermediaries with the Indian merchants and British engineers and survey officers, who themselves crop up in the text.

Turning from the author to the text itself, it is worth first laying out a few basic details of its composition and format. At some fifty-seven pages of lithographic print, the *Safarnama-e Uganda* was of fairly typical length for its genre and period. Printed in Lahore in one of North India's most important publishing centers—and certainly the most important in Punjab—it was printed in the lithographic format that preserved the handwritten look of a manuscript, while in a reflection of the technologies transforming the Indian Ocean at large was printed on a steam press to ensure its cheap and large-scale reproduction. As such, the edition was a classic example of South Asian cheap print. Like other Urdu travel texts of its period, the *Safarnama-e Uganda* blended practical information and advice with bursts of lyrical and at times exoticizing description, often at the expense of various African peoples who were regularly described as "wild" (*wahshi*).[32] This curious compromise between what in English would be seen as the distinct genres of the practical travel guide and the literary travelogue characterized many such texts of the period, balanced as they were between an early period of the more embellished and literary Persian *safarnama*, when few readers would actually undertake similar journeys themselves, and the Victorian era of the Urdu *safarnama*, when large numbers of South Asians were on the move via train and steamship. In line with pre-colonial Persian *safarnamas*, the author of the *Safarnama-e Uganda* thus made repeated recourse to poetic praise of the flowers, trees, and gardens of East Africa: even though "it is hard for my pen to find the power to describe the area's qualities, the view is a heart-arresting sight . . . it is as though a green velvet carpet had been rolled out into the distance brought to life by red, rose, yellow and white flowers."[33]

The peoples of East Africa and their unfamiliar customs were in

---

[32] For fuller discussion, see Green, "Africa in Indian Ink."

[33] *Safarnāma (1904),* 17. On the conventions of the pre-colonial Persian *safarnama* in India, see M. Alam and S. Subrahmanyam, *Indo-Persian Travels in the Age of Discoveries, 1400–1800* (Cambridge, Eng.: Cambridge University Press, 2007).

places similarly framed in terms of the pre-colonial *safarnama* category of the "weird and wonderful" (*'ajib u gharib*).[34] Such stories had long been told about Africa and its surrounding maritime regions, not least in Munshi I'tisam al-Din's late eighteenth-century Indo-Persian travelogue *Shigarfnama-e Wilayat* (*Book of the Wonders of the Homeland*), which in its account of the Indian Ocean described the seas around the island of Kaf (presumably La Réunion or perhaps Mauritius) as rolling with boiling waves that killed every sailor who came into contact with them.[35] Just as the earlier *safarnama* writers had recounted yarns of strange and in some cases legendary beasts, the author of the *Safarnama-e Uganda* devoted a special section to "animals not found in India," with long sections passing on a blend of fact and folklore concerning the ostrich (*shotar-morgh*, literally "camel bird"), zebra (*zibra*), giraffe (*jiraf*), and rhinoceros (*ginda* or *gorg-shir*, literally "wolf-lion").[36] Elsewhere in the text the author recounted a version of the story of the "Lions of Tsavo," the incident made famous in John Henry Paterson's 1907 *Maneaters of Tsavo* in which up to 135 South Asian railway workers were killed by lions before the predators were culled by British officers and hunters.[37] If these lions were not as fantastical as the *izhdiha* or "dragon" that in the 1913 hagiography discussed in the next section was said to have terrified the first South Asian settlers in Natal, then the animals nonetheless belonged to the same generic conventions of the pre-colonial *safarnama* of highlighting the exotic and strange.[38]

While no doubt informed by the author's own readings in the Urdu literature of travel, in the *Safarnama-e Uganda* such generic flourishes were balanced and ultimately outweighed by the more practical forms of information that the author sought to pass on to his readership of potential migrants. From the very first pages of the travelogue, the author repeatedly

[34] *Safarnāma (1904),* 25–26, 30, 34–36, 40.

[35] Munshī I'tisām al-Dīn, *Shigarfnāma-e Wilāyat,* Urdu translation by Amīr Hasan Nūrānī (Patna: Khoda Baksh Public Library, 1995), 31–32. For further discussion of this and other maritime travelogues, see N. S. Green, "Saints, Rebels and Booksellers: Sufis in the Cosmopolitan Western Indian Ocean, c. 1850–1920," in *Struggling with History: Islam and Cosmopolitanism in the Western Indian Ocean,* ed. K. Kresse and E. Simpson (New York: Columbia University Press, 2007).

[36] *Safarnāma (1904),* 51–54.

[37] Ibid., 51; and J. H. Paterson, *Maneaters of Tsavo and Other East African Adventures* (London: Macmillan, 1907). On the incident, see also Metcalf, *Imperial Connections,* 202–3.

[38] Shaykh Dā'ūd bin Sulaymān, *Riyāz-e Sūfī* (Bombay: Mustafā'ī Steam Press, 1331/1913), 11–12.

stressed that his account of Africa was not a "fairy tale" (*qissa*) or a "story" (*kahani*), but what he had seen with his own eyes and heard with his own ears. It was a claim reemphasized on the book's cover, where the contents were described as the "eyewitness conditions (*chasm-did halat*)" of life in East Africa.[39] This epistemology of directly verified knowledge of foreign places had already begun to emerge in the Persian and Indo-Persian travelogues in the earlier nineteenth century in response to the growing number of travelers demanding reliable information.[40] That information was of course presented in the discursive and conceptual terms of the Islamic *safarnama*, while also drawing strongly on various colonial attitudes toward Africa that were more contemporary with its composition. For in its widely ranging contents, the *Safarnama-e Uganda* provided ethnographic accounts of various East African "tribes" (*qawm*), which ranged from relatively appreciative depictions of Muslim Swahili to picturesque descriptions of the folk dances and customs of peoples of the interior that in some cases drew on stereotypes of African peoples as "wild" (*wahshi*) and "naked" (*birahna*) jungle-dwellers who lacked civilization (*tamaddun*) and refused to follow the laws of any of God's prophets.[41] In similar vein, by drawing on both long-standing stereotypes and more contemporary colonial representations of Africa, the *Safarnama-e Uganda* also recounted "strange" (*'ajib*) tales of "magicians" (*jadugar*) and lost African cities.[42] Moving from the fantastical to claims of fact, the text presented an outline of East African history in which Arab Muslim settlers were given a central role in bringing civilization to the "bloodthirsty" (*khunkhwar*) indigenes who dwelt in caves and forests.[43] Depicting the British as the continuers of this civilizing process, the text was entirely positive in its depiction of British rule in the region.[44] In dating from 1901, the *Safarnama-e Uganda* therefore preserves a richly detailed if in places disturbing summary of the ways in which at least some South Asian settlers understood and related to their new African environment in the very first years of mass South Asian migration to East Africa.

---

[39] *Safarnāma* (1904), 4, 5.

[40] On the new epistemology of travel, see N. S. Green, "Among the Dissenters: Reciprocal Ethnography in Nineteenth Century Inglistan," *Journal of Global History* 4, no. 2 (2009).

[41] *Safarnāma* (1904), 24–26, 29–35, 43–50.

[42] Ibid., 40, 46, 48–49.

[43] Ibid., 6–11.

[44] Ibid., 11–12.

The *Safarnama-e Uganda wa Mumbasa* was by no means the only Urdu travel account to have been written about the region, and it can be usefully counterposed with one of the several post-colonial travelogues of the later twentieth century.[45] The *safarnama* continued to be an important genre of Urdu engagement with Africa in the decades after South Asian and East African independence, not least in recording the journeys of Muslim religious scholars. The text to which we will turn in more detail for the next sample study is the travelogue of the Karachi-based religious scholar Manzur Husayn Mahir al-Qadiri (1906–1978).[46] The latter was a well-known Indian (and later Pakistani) writer of Urdu short stories (*afsana*) and lyrical poetry (*ghazal*) who was also highly regarded for his skills as a preacher and reciter of praise poems (*na'at*).[47] It was this renown that in 1969 brought Mahir al-Qadiri an invitation to Durban from the Nazdil Quran Council, one of the numerous South Asian Muslim religious organizations that were active in South Africa by this period. While Mahir al-Qadiri therefore never actually lived in Africa, to see him as merely a visiting Pakistani interloper would be to miss the larger point about the interconnections and circulations of Islamic literatures between South Asia and Africa. For while born in the village of Kesar Kalan in the Bulandshahr district of the United Provinces of northern India, after studying at Aligarh Muslim University, he later moved to the princely state of Hyderabad before migrating to Pakistan shortly after its foundation in 1947. As early as 1933 he had crossed the Indian Ocean to travel to Baghdad and the holy sites of Iraq, and while from 1947 he spent much of his remaining twenty years in Karachi, he continued to travel widely, making the hajj in 1953 and additional tours of the Hijaz, Egypt, Turkey, Lebanon, and much of Europe in 1969 and 1976. When he died, he was buried in Mecca rather than in Pakistan. In the case of each of his journeys, Mahir al-Qadiri wrote Urdu travelogues, such as his 1954 *Karwan-e Hijaz* (*Hijaz Caravan*), often compiled from letters he sent home.[48] As both lived and written, his life was

---

[45] For a study of a post-colonial Gujarati travelogue from 1972, see Basu, "Politics of Travelling."

[46] Manzūr Husayn Māhir al-Qādirī, *Siyāhat-Nāma-e Māhir al-Qādirī* (Lahore: Hasānat Akādimī, 1987).

[47] On the author's life, see 'Abd al-Ghanī Fārūq, "*Muqadima*," in Māhir al-Qādirī, *Siyāhat-Nāma-e Māhir al-Qādirī,* 8–12; and 'Abd al-Ghanī Fārūq, *Māhir al-Qādirī: Hayāt ū Adabī Khidamāt* (Lahore: Idāra-e Ma'ārif-e Islāmī-e Mansūra, 2002).

[48] Manzūr Husayn Māhir al-Qādirī, *Kārwān-e Hijāz* (Delhi: Markazī Maktaba-ye Jamā'at Islāmī-ye Hind, repr. 1966).

therefore one that was not narrowly Pakistani or even South Asian, but one that belonged to a larger arena, both oceanic and Islamic, that brought together South Asia and South Africa with Egypt and Arabia.

Written in fine literary style, the epistolary travelogue of Mahir al-Qadiri's 1969 African journey captures well this interconnected geography. For its accounts of Durban, Johannesburg, Cape Town, Nairobi, and Mombasa occur as part of the larger journey to Istanbul, Beirut, and ultimately Mecca that were also depicted. In being constructed from a sequence of letters written to his younger brother in Karachi, the travelogue not only conformed to a larger oceanic genre of the letter collection that we have seen earlier in Narasimbhai Ishwarbhai Patel's Gujarati *Africa na Pathro* (*Letters from Africa*). It also inserted itself into African literature in comprising letters that Mahir al-Qadiri actually wrote in such cities as Mombasa and Durban. As we will see below with regard to the letters exchanged between Ghulam Muhammad in Durban and Habibullah Shah in Bombay, such epistolary networks appear to have been particularly important in the development of a public sphere in Urdu no less than other African languages in this period. As Keith Breckenridge has noted (drawing on Isaac Schapera) with regard to the expansion of letter-writing among South African Xhosa-speakers during the early twentieth century, letters "offer an unmatched opportunity for inquisitive social scientists to explore the hidden world of African consciousness."[49]

In this way, Mahir al-Qadiri's *safarnama* was both travelogue and letter collection, a fusion of two important genres of writing on Africa. As well as pointing to the travelogue's versatility and longevity as a genre on Indo-African interactions, it documents a later point in the process of South Asian settlement in Africa than that described in the *Safarnama-e Uganda*. In contrast to its predecessor, in Mahir al-Qadiri's travelogue there were no disparaging depictions of Africans. Indeed, after almost a century of South Asian immigration, black Africans could now almost be sidelined from the depiction of Africa. For in Mahir al-Qadiri's account, the cities of Kenya and South Africa appeared as flourishing centers of South Asian life. While the *Safarnama-e Uganda* opens up the lost perceptions that early South Asian settlers had of Africans, Mahir al-Qadiri's travelogue brings to life the social world of South Asians themselves in Africa. His letters presented

---

[49] K. Breckenridge, "Reasons for Writing: African Working-Class Letter-Writing in Early Twentieth-Century South Africa," in *Africa's Hidden Histories: Everyday Literacy and Making the Self*, ed. K. Barber (Bloomington: Indiana University Press, 2006), 144.

sketches of South Asian African notables (*ahbab*), such as businessmen and literary figures, many of whom were presented as attending the Urdu classes taught at mosques in Nairobi, Durban, and Johannesburg.[50]

This sense of the living presence of Urdu in Africa is heightened by Mahir al-Qadiri's accounts of several *musha'ira*, the poetry gatherings that provide the social architecture of Urdu literature.[51] Adapting the old literary tropes to the African environment, his travelogue recorded an Urdu poem on the subject of springtime (*bahar*) in Durban.[52] The travelogue also lends a sense of South Asia and Africa as connected geographies through such episodes as the author encountering an old acquaintance in Durban whom he had last met at a meeting of the Muslim League in Nagpur in 1942 or seeing another acquaintance in Nairobi whom he had previously known in Karachi.[53] Almost presenting Nairobi as a South Asian city, Mahir al-Qadiri described the Kenyan city as replete with South Asian social clubs and mosques, factories and literary circles.[54] But while this was clearly a more Asianized Africa than that of the *Safarnama-e Uganda* of almost seventy years earlier, the two travelogues still shared certain preoccupations. There was much practical detail on African infrastructure, trade, and industries, such as South Africa's gold mines.[55] Like its predecessor, Mahir al-Qadiri's account contained evocative if stylized depictions of Africa's natural beauty and animal life.[56] Moreover, the later text also sought commonalities through the idioms of a shared Islamic heritage. For as well as comparing the mosques of Karachi, Durban, and Nairobi, Mahir al-Qadiri also included in his letters home a discussion of the commonalities bequeathed to Urdu and Swahili by a joint Islamic and Arabic history.[57] It was a point he emphasized through an Urdu/Swahili vocabulary in which he selected words from both languages that had the same Arabic origin. Bringing these Islamic ties up to date, he also related how at the University of Witwatersrand, the Department of Islamic Studies was teaching the Urdu poetry of Muhammad Iqbal.[58]

---

[50] Māhir al-Qādirī, *Siyāhat-Nāma-e Māhir al-Qādirī,* 59.

[51] Ibid., 58–59, 75–76.

[52] Ibid., 58.

[53] Ibid., 58, 73.

[54] On the Kenyan section, see ibid., 57–60 and 70–83.

[55] Ibid., 40–44.

[56] Ibid., 71–74.

[57] Ibid., 80–81.

[58] Ibid., 38–39.

Mahir al-Qadiri was only one of many South Asian Muslim scholars to tour South and East Africa in the years after the opening of regular air routes between the regions. From the 1960s, a whole series of Deobandi scholars made preaching tours of South Africa, including Qari Muhammad Tayyib (1963), Muhammad Shafi' and Ihtisham al-Haqq (1966), Muhammad Palan Haqqani (1969), and Mahmud Hasan Gangohi (1990).[59] In some instances, these tours resulted in formal travel accounts, as in the case of Ashfaq Ahmad Bahriabadi (1900–1981) and the Deobandi scholar and Chishti Sufi Muhammad Zakariya al-Kandhlawi (1898–1982).[60] Written by his disciples Muhammad Shahid and Najib Allah, the two travelogues of Muhammad Zakariya depict a journey to South Africa, Reunion, Zambia, and on to England that took place in 1981.[61] His travelogues are highly stylized documents in which the acts and itineraries of travel are secondary to the expounding of spiritual lessons and moral admonitions. The journey was in this way embedded in a master narrative of saintly biography in which Muhammad Zakariya's travels were surrounded with dreams of the Prophet Muhammad and "revelations" (*basharat*) that the journey unveiled.[62] In this respect, the texts have much in common with the hagiographical works discussed in the next section. Moreover, Muhammad Shahid's account of the African journey contained almost no details of the journey's African locations and instead provided a narrative of praying, blessings, signs of respect, deferential meetings, and moral discussions. Even specific places were presented not as cities but as social networks: Durban, for example, featured in the text solely as a circle of

[59] Thanks to Brannon Ingram for this information.

[60] Qāzī Ashfāq Ahmad Bahrīābādī (with 'Abd al-Khalāq Shawkat, *Safarnāma-ye Afrīqa* (Lucknow: Taqsīmkār Dānish Mahal, 1987); and Muftī Muhammad Shāhid and Najīb Allāh, *Qutb al-Aqtāb Imām al-'Ārifīn Shaykh al-Mashā'ikh Hazrat Aqdas Shaykh al-Hadīs al-Hājj al-Hāfiz Mawlānā Muhammad Zakariyā Muhājir Madanī kā Safarnāma-ye Afrīqah wa Inglaind, Ramazān al-Mubārak 1401H./1981'I* (Karachi: Al-Maktabat al-Islāmiya, 1982).

[61] The published edition of Muhammad Shāhid and Najīb Allāh's *Qutb al-Aqtāb* in fact comprises five texts, with Muhammad Shāhid's account of the African journey on pp. 9–46; Najīb Allāh's account of the South African, Zambian, and English journeys on pp. 47–150; a commentary by Munawwar Husayn on the African journey on pp. 151–57; an account of Muhammad Zariya's school on pp. 158–66; and a summary of translated newspaper reports on his journeys on pp. 167–73.

[62] On the dreams and revelations, see, e.g., Muhammad Shāhid and Najīb Allāh, *Qutb al-Aqtāb,* 16–17, 45–46.

mosques and pious Muslims.[63] In this travelogue at least, Africa was not so much meaningful in itself but as a crucible of Deobandi piety.

In Najib Allah's account of Muhammad Zakariya's visit to Zambia the journey itself does feature, though again almost to the exclusion of the locations visited: Najib Allah recounted a minute-by-minute breakdown of the itinerary of roads, car changes, prayer stops, airports, suitcase collecting, *durud* chanting, and ticket purchasing. Once again the destination was a Zambia of mosques and prayer meetings.[64] Prompted by an invitation from an Islamic Center on the island whose director was one of Muhammad Zakariya's disciples, Muhammad Shahid's short account of the visit to Réunion similarly revolved around the limited geography of an Islamic religious network.[65] Yet the fact that these travelogues are not accounts of exotic African customs or safari wildlife in no way undermines their relationship with Africa. Instead, it points to the way in which Urdu materials reveal the semantic and social pluralities of the continent. For what the travelogues of Muhammad Shahid and Najib Allah reveal is a South Asian Muslim community in Africa which (in its depiction at least) is wholly self-contained and self-referential. For Muhammad Zakariya and his party, Africa is absorbed without question into a globalized conception of an "Islamic world" in which such luminaries as Muhammad Zakariya are as welcome in Johannesburg as they are in La Réunion and London. Globalized rather than colonized, and familiarly Islamic rather than strangely semi-civilized, by 1981 this was quite another Africa from that depicted in the 1901 *Safarnama-ye Uganda wa Mumbasa*.

As we have seen with Muhammad Zakariya's Urdu preaching in Zambia, in other cases too the greater mobility of the later twentieth century saw Urdu expand into new regions of Africa. An earlier example is the travelogue of the 1970s preaching tour of Ahmad Canyuti and Khalid Mahmud that encompassed Kenya, Ghana, Sierra Leone, Gambia, and Nigeria as part of an effort to expand into West Africa the Ahmadiya version of Islam that had emerged in nineteenth-century Punjab.[66] In this way,

[63] Muhammad Shāhid and Najīb Allāh, *Qutb al-Aqtāb*, 34–36. A list of actual towns (more specifically mosques) visited in South Africa does finally appear on p. 44.

[64] Muhammad Shāhid and Najīb Allāh, *Qutb al-Aqtāb,* 77–102, especially 77–82 on the travel itinerary.

[65] Muhammad Shāhid and Najīb Allāh, *Qutb al-Aqtāb,* 31–34.

[66] Muhammad Siddīq Amritsarī, *Rūh Parwar Yādēn, ya'nī Sayyidinā Hazrat Imām-e Jamā'at-e Ahmadiyya kē Shāndār Tablīghī Dawra-yi Maghribī Afrīqa 1970 kī Rūdād* (Lahore: Muhammad Latīf Anvar Amritsarī, 1981). On the earlier expansion of the Ahmadiya

the global rather than the colonial reach of Urdu points to the broadening relevance of the language for other regions of Africa beyond its initial footholds in Durban and Mombasa.

The Hagiography

Biographies of saints and scholars had circulated the Indian Ocean long before the emergence of the modern South Asian communities in East and South Africa. Connecting the older tropes of the genre to the newer experiences of colonial South Asian settlement in Africa was the Urdu hagiography of Ghulam Muhammad 'Sufi Sahib' (d. 1911).[67] Having been raised in a small town on the Konkan littoral of western India, before his relocation to Durban in the mid-1890s Ghulam Muhammad had first migrated to Bombay and entered the fellowship of the Hyderabadi Sufi master Habib 'Ali Shah (d. 1906). Following on the trail of the indentured laborers who became the mass of his followers and the merchant "passenger Indians" who became his patrons, in the course of around fifteen years in South Africa Ghulam Muhammad was able to establish an efficient network of mosques and madrasa schools throughout Natal in which the teaching of Urdu played a central part in the curriculum. On his death in 1911, he was buried in the large mausoleum built for him on the outskirts of Durban and it was as part of the larger enshrinement process that a hagiography was commissioned for his followers in Natal. Drawing on the conventions of the older genre of the Islamic hagiography (*tabaqa*, *tazkira*), *Riyaz-e Sufi* was more part of a larger oceanic literary culture than a new introduction to Africa of a discrete South Asian genre. Issued in 1913 as a cheap print pamphlet, *Riyaz-e Sufi* (*Travails of the Sufi*) described Ghulam Muhammad's traumatic oceanic steamship travels and his travails of settling in South Africa.[68] Appropriately enough in view of the steam-powered entanglements of the entire process of Urdu's expansion into Africa, this short book was printed for the South African market on the Mustafa'i

---

into the region, see H. J. Fisher, *Ahmadiyyah: A Study in Contemporary Islām on the West African Coast* (London: Oxford University Press, 1963).

[67] For fuller discussion of Ghulam Muhammad's career, see N. S. Green, "Islam for the Indentured Indian: A Muslim Missionary in Colonial South Africa," *Bulletin of the School of Oriental and African Studies* 71, no. 3 (2008).

[68] Shaykh Dā'ūd bin Sulaymān, *Riyāz-e Sūfī*. For a more detailed study of the text, see Green, "Dilemmas of the Pious Biographer."

Steam Press of Bombay, a city that we have already seen exporting books in a range of other "oceanic" and "African" languages.

In making sense of these Indo-African exchanges, it is worth taking a closer look at the authorial history of *Riyaz-e Sufi*. Shaykh Da'ud, the formal author, recorded the stories he had heard from Tajammul Husayn, an Indian follower of Ghulam Muhammad's brother-in-law and deputy, 'Abd al-Latif. While the latter had followed Ghulam Muhammad to South Africa, Shaykh Da'ud and Tajammul Husayn appear to have remained in Bombay, from where they were commissioned to write the hagiography by Ghulam Muhammad's followers in Natal. In contrast to the travelogues discussed in the previous section which were actually written *in* Africa, we are here dealing with a text that was written *for* Africa. However, to regard *Riyaz-e Sufi* on these grounds as being an "Indian" rather than an "African" text would be to miss the key point about the oceanic circulation of literary cultures between Africa and South Asia, particularly in the era of mass labor migration from which it emerged. Moreover, Urdu had no more a natural or historical home in Bombay than it had in Durban, and the language reached both cities as a result of the labor migrations of the nineteenth century. The connected ports of Durban and Bombay were in this way twin partners in the trans-regional expansion of Urdu in the late nineteenth century. The writer/reader balancing of the two cities put in place by the book's composition in Bombay and reception in Durban captures well the interdependence of the two regions as part of a larger and expanding literary sphere.

The actual contents of *Riyaz-e Sufi* reinforce these points, for the biography of Ghulam Muhammad it contains constructed a life history between South Asia and Africa. Following the classic formulas of the Islamic biography, the text described the family background, education, and spiritual initiation of its subject, before turning to his travels (in this case, to South Africa) and his miraculous victories (in this case, against his enemies in Natal), before finally detailing his death and burial (in a grand mausoleum outside Durban). In terms of content as much as its authorship and reception, we are therefore dealing with a text that moved multiply between South Africa and South Asia, as the very stories from which it was woven had first been told in Durban before being carried across the ocean to Bombay before being printed there and shipped back to Durban. In following the movements of its writers and audience, *Riyaz-e Sufi* also reflected the letters that similarly moved between continents, whether as the constituent parts of Urdu travelogues (such as Mahir al-Qadiri's) or

Gujarati letter collections (such as Ishwarbhai Patel's). While they have never been published, there survives among Ghulam Muhammad's descendants in Natal a collection of Urdu correspondence that he exchanged from Durban with his sheikh, Habibullah Shah, in Bombay.[69] What Vukile Khumalo has written of Ekukhanyeni letter exchanges in the South Africa of this period could also be applied to the letters sent between Ghulam Muhammad and Habibullah Shah: "The letter constituted a space for discussion and dreaming. Letter-writers valued those who knew how to write and encouraged the novice."[70] While this article's survey is limited to printed materials that are more readily available to scholars, there is no doubt that many more such unpublished Urdu materials are preserved by East and South African Asian families.

As to the question as to whether *Riyaz-e Sufi* finally "belonged" in one place more than another—whether like various texts in time it eventually settled for a particular home—then the answer would have to be in South Africa rather than South Asia. For like all such hagiographical writings, *Riyaz-e Sufi* was the textual companion of its subject's shrine. The mausoleum made no sense without its stories, just as its stories made no sense without the shrine, a point reinforced by the hymns printed in the book's final pages to be sung at the Durban shrine. It was there, rather than in Bombay, that the text was preserved and eventually reprinted in the original Urdu in 2001.

Poetry and Historical Writings

Beyond the genres of the travelogue and hagiography, in a reflection of the late arrival of printing in India, Urdu literary culture had never relied solely or even mainly on written texts and it was the poetry recital party or *musha'ira* which served as the main social occasion for the sharing of Urdu poetry.[71] Reaching their peak of sophistication and prestige in India only in the nineteenth century, by the twentieth century *musha'ira* were

[69] The Durban-based descendants of Ghulam Muhammad have generously provided me with a copy of this letter collection.

[70] V. Khumalo, "Ekukhanyeni Letter-Writers: An Historical Enquiry into Epistolary Network(s) and Political Imagination in Kwazulu-Natal, South Africa," in Barber (2006), 121.

[71] On *musha'ira* in the context of the other oral literatures of East African Asians, see M. Hassanali Kirmani and S. Kirmani, *Oral Literature of the Asians in East Africa* (Nairobi: East African Publishers, 2002), 19–20.

being informally established in Mombasa and Nairobi, as well as in Natal, with formal Urdu literary associations being established by the 1930s, such as the two Bazm-e Adab organizations founded in Durban in 1932 and Nairobi in 1937 by Hajji Aslam Chishti.[72] Given the importance of Urdu lyrical poetry to the agricultural laborers and railway builders who migrated from the United Provinces and Punjab in the late nineteenth century, it would seem safe to assume that Urdu poetry flourished orally in informal *musha'ira* settings before such formal organizations were established. However, we have as yet little record of the poetry composed or performed in this earlier period, and in his Urdu account of the language's history in East Africa, Kalidas Gupta Riza states that no collections (*majmu'a*) survive from before the 1930s.[73]

Further research among surviving members of Nairobi and Durban's Urdu literary associations might well bring to light anthologies or literary magazines from the 1930s and 1940s. However, research for this article has only brought to light more recent anthologies published in the 1970s and 1980s, albeit including poetry written in earlier decades as well. Among the more important of these later anthologies of African Urdu is *Pardes Hamara Des* (*Abroad Is Our Home*), which has brought together the verse of three self-identifying Kenyan Urdu poets from the mid-twentieth century.[74] Included among the three poets was Wasim Butt 'Wasim,' who in reflection of East Africa's earlier connections with Urdu via Punjab was born in the Punjabi city of Sialkot in 1946. After graduating from Punjab University in 1968, Wasim Butt emigrated to Kenya in 1974 and as well as writing in the classical forms of the *ghazal* (lyric) and *ruba'i* (quatrain) devoted much of his time to the practical promotion of Urdu.[75] Another valuable collection is Imdad Sabiri's *Junubi Afriqa ke Urdu Sha'ir* (*South Africa's Urdu Poets*), which has provided extensive contextual and biographical data on South African Urdu poets as well as samples of their writing.[76] Such has been the scale of Urdu poetic production in Africa that a subsidiary field of literary criticism has begun to emerge around it,

[72] Anonymous, "Origin and Development of Islam and Islamic Education in South Africa Since the Seventeenth Century," typescript, Durban Cultural and Documentation Centre, file Religion: Islam (95/173) and Kālīdās Guptā Rizā, *Bahār-e Urdū,* 37.

[73] Kālīdās Guptā Rizā, *Bahār-e Urdū,* 36.

[74] Anjum 'Abbās, *Pardēs Hamāra Dēs: Kēnyā (Mashriqī Afrīqa) kē Tīn Mashhūr Shā'irūn kā Muntakhab Kalām* (Bombay: Kokan Writers Guild, 1989).

[75] Ibid., 15–16.

[76] Imdād Sābirī, *Junūbī Afrīqa kē Urdū Shā'ir* (Delhi: Sābirī Akādimī, 1978).

such as the study written by the Pakistani poet and critic Naqqash Kazmi (1944–).[77]

Prose works have also continued to be an important feature of African Urdu, particularly by way of historical and biographical accounts of the founders of the South Asian communities in Africa. Two of the most important examples are the aforementioned *Bahar-e Urdu Gulshan-e Mashriqi Afriqa Men* (*Urdu Springtime in the Rose Garden of East Africa*) and *Hindustani Mashriqi Afriqa Men* (*Indians in East Africa*), both written by Kalidas Gupta Riza (1925–2001), a prolific Urdu scholar who like so many East African migrants was himself born in the Punjabi city of Jalandhar and based for much of his life in Mombasa's South Asian twin city of Bombay.[78] As we have seen earlier, *Bahar-e Urdu* provided a detailed history of the development of Urdu in East Africa from 1899 until the 1980s, weaving around this literary theme a larger narrative of South Asian achievements in the region. Opening up a post-colonial South Asian perspective on African history, *Bahar-e Urdu* placed South Asians (and particularly Punjabis) at the heart of modern East African history; it is a narrative of South Asian pioneers and British followers.[79] In similar vein, the main focus of Kalidas Gupta Riza's *Hindustani Mashriqi Afriqa Men* is on the biographies of the South Asian "founding fathers" of East Africa. There is a particular focus on merchants such as Jai Ram Shuji (1790–1866) and 'Ali Dinawsaram (1863–1916), but the text also deals with leading lawyers and public servants.[80] Here as throughout Kalidas Gupta Riza's writings was the claim that it was South Asians who effectively civilized East Africa through their fearlessness and hard work, settling its "terrifying and wild mountainous interior" (*andaruni khawfnak jangali pahari*) and "deserted quarters" (*wayran 'alaqun*).[81]

Other Urdu accounts of Africa place prominence on the centrality of Islam in African history, using religion as a means to bring together the history of African and South Asian peoples. A notable example is Muhammad

[77] Naqqāsh Kāzmī, *Afrō-Eshiyā'ī Adībōn kē Masā'il aur unkā pas Manzar* (Karachi: Gulcihrah Ikaidamī, 1986).

[78] Kālīdās Guptā Rizā *Bahār-e Urdū;* and Kālīdās Guptā Rizā, *Hindustānī Mashriqī Afrīqa Men* (Bombay: Vimal, 1977).

[79] Kālīdās Guptā Rizā, *Bahār-e Urdū,* 18.

[80] On Shuji and Dinawsaram, see Kālīdās Guptā Rizā, *Hindustānī Mashriqī Afrīqa Men,* 47–56 and 57–66 respectively.

[81] Kālīdās Guptā Rizā, *Bahār-e Urdū,* 18.

Faruqi's study of the spread of Islam throughout Africa, which ranges from the early Islamic period until the 1980s.[82] Faruqi's book is notable for the comprehensiveness of its vision, ranging from the early arrival of Arab Muslims to the activities of the Sanusi Sufis in Libya to the more recent preaching tours of scholars from the Indian seminary at Deoband, in this way linking the activities of modern South Asian Muslims to a much older lineage of Muslim pietists in Africa. Another prominent feature of Faruqi's text is its attention to the different peoples (*aqwam*) of Africa, which includes Indians (*hindustani*) alongside Berbers, Arabs, and Bantu and other "Negro" (*negro*) peoples.[83] In Faruqi's discussion of the languages (*zibanen*) of Africa, emphasis is placed on Arabic as the provider of the script and much of the vocabulary for various African languages such as Somali and Hausa.[84] By making comparisons with the way this process also shaped the evolution of Urdu, the latter was implicitly linked to a larger family of Islamic languages in both Africa and Asia that all "descended" from Arabic.[85]

As we have seen in such works as Kalidas Gupta Riza's *Hindustāni Mashriqī Afrīqa Men*, the Urdu historiography of Africa certainly contains stereotypes that draw on the clichés of colonial attitudes to Africa, stereotypes that were also found in colonial South Asian writings in English about Africa from the early twentieth century.[86] These stereotypes and tropes are important, for they open up the discursive contours of South Asian interactions with Africa that reveal the possibilities of more nuanced critical studies of social interaction across the Indian Ocean. Nonetheless, as we have seen with Muhammad Faruqi's *Afriqa aur Khidmat Faqih al-Ummat*, Urdu historiography also provides insight into the conceptual apparatus by which South Asia and Africa are connected as part of a unitary Islamic space. This collapsing of continents into a singular Islamic world is also a development we have noted in other genres, such as the 1981 travelogues of Muhammad Zakariya.

[82] Muhammad Fārūqī, *Afrīqa aur Khidmāt Faqīh al-Ummat* (Deoband: Maktaba Nashr al-Mahmūd, 1411/1991). Thanks to Brannon Ingram for supplying me with a copy of this text.

[83] Ibid., 28–30; on Indians, see ibid., 30.

[84] Ibid., 30–35.

[85] Ibid., 34–35. Thanks again to Brannon Ingram for pointing me to this reference.

[86] I. Hofmeyr, "The Idea of 'Africa' in Indian Nationalism: Reporting the Diaspora in *The Modern Review*, 1907–1929," *South African Historical Journal* 57 (2007).

Conclusions

The main aim of this article has been to sketch the outlines of an unrecognized source literature in the hope that it will encourage further research into Urdu materials for the study of African, Indo-African, or Indian Ocean history. Through brief sample studies of a range of genres, we have seen that the scope of Urdu in Africa has not been limited to a few random books but has instead constituted a variety of genres that range from travelogues, letter collections, and hagiographies to poetry collections and historical works. The sample studies provided here are in no way meant to hint at comprehensiveness and, with the exception of the works discussed in the hagiography section, all of these texts have been located in such research libraries as the British Library, the Library of Congress, and the libraries of the University of Chicago and the University of California, Berkeley. While African and South Asian libraries surely contain many more examples of African Urdu in such well-established genres as the travelogue and lyrical poem, it is hoped that committed researchers will bring to light works in such other genres as the letter collection (*maktubat*) and short story (*afsana*), as well as unpublished manuscript texts and documents of a non-literary kind. Perhaps most important, the Urdu journals and newspapers that expanded rapidly in the later nineteenth century also seem likely sources of untapped early accounts of Indian settlement in Africa. Since languages of other South Asian settler groups in Africa may also have developed similar literary records, further research may uncover Hindi or Punjabi African literatures that emerged in parallel to that in Urdu. There do, for example, exist several Hindi travelogues written in the 1920s by Indian supporters of Gandhi, such as Bhavanidayala Sannyasi (1893–1950).[87]

While the emphasis here has largely been on the potential for historical research, the ongoing and indeed expanding place of Urdu in Africa suggests that anthropological and sociological research also have much to benefit from these materials. Among the more interesting recent developments is the use of Urdu as a means of interaction between different regions of Africa rather than between Africa and South Asia, a development seen in the Urdu translation of the prizewinning West African Mami

[87] Bhavānīdayāla Sannyāsī, *Dakshiṇa Afrikā ke mere Anubhava: Pravāsī-bhāīyoṃ kī Sāmājika Tathā Rājanītika daśā kā Digdarśana* (Allahabad: Cānda Kāryālaya, 1927); and Bhavānīdayāla Sannyāsī, *Dakshiṇa Aphrikā ke Satyāgrahkā Itihāsa Sacitra* (Indore: Sarasvatī-Sadana, 1920).

Wata children's stories written by the Johannesburg-based Côte d'Ivoire author Véronique Tadjo (1955–).[88] The aim of this article, though, has not been to make any specific interpretive or historical arguments in relation to what such source materials can and cannot demonstrate. However, it is clear that such literary sources present the possibilities of writing cultural, connected, or subaltern histories of the kind that the reliance on colonial archives and other English-language sources has largely precluded.

Insofar as there has been an argument in the previous pages, it has been to reposition Urdu as an "African language." It is therefore worth concluding with a clarification of what kind of claim this is. For in pointing to the importance and availability of Urdu sources on life in Africa, the aim has not been to enter futile debates on where languages "belong" and insofar as this essay has used a conceptual model of language history, it has been one of oceanic rather than national or continental literary cultures. People move, and with them move languages and literatures in turn. Against this background, in the previous pages we have seen the longevity of Urdu's presence in Africa, a presence that can arguably be dated back to the first arrival of North Indian laborers in Natal in the 1860s. In this respect, the length of Urdu's presence in Africa can be compared to that of English in California and Yiddish in New York, or in an Indian Ocean context, to the presence of Tamil in Malaysia. For the great migrations of the nineteenth-century steam age rapidly restructured the planet's linguistic geography. It can certainly be argued that the category of "African language" should properly be reserved for languages that have achieved a critical mass of speakers among a wider population. But while Urdu is admittedly not a language of cross-ethnic usage (except among different Indian groups), then the same might also be said of Afrikaans.[89] Moreover, temporal longevity and literary production are surely also important criteria. It is worth bearing in mind that Urdu has a longer presence in parts of Africa than it does in parts of Pakistan, where it is nonetheless considered the official language. Decisions on where languages "belong" are therefore always based on partial or arbitrary criteria. If Urdu reached Africa through the linguistic circulations of an oceanic culture zone, then in the course of a century and a half it has also put down roots in solid ground. Rich in undiscovered sources, Urdu's legacy in Africa should be taken seriously by all who recognize the plurality of Africa's pasts.

---

[88] V. Tadjō, *Māmī Wātā aur Khawfnāk Dīv,* trans. Gulshan Iqbāl (London: Millet, 2000).

[89] Thanks to Christopher Ehret for this point.

The Promotion of Sufism in the Politics of Algeria and Morocco

*Fait Muedini,** ECKERD COLLEGE

DOI: 10.5192/215409930302201

ABSTRACT

This paper examines the promotion of Sufism by government leaders in Algeria and Morocco. Specifically, this paper finds that both Abdelaziz Bouteflika of Algeria and Mohammed VI of Morocco have each emphasized Sufi Islam in a number of manners that include but are not limited to public media statements about the value of Sufism in society, as well as voicing support with regard to organizing conferences on Sufism. But while such actions are often carried out in the name of combating religious extremism, statements made about Sufism by such leaders also seem to suggest that they may be operating under the assumption that Sufis are either apolitical and thus are not seen as a threat, or that Sufism can be used to counter Islamist organizations that are politically challenging to the government.

Keywords: Sufism; Islam; North Africa; Middle East; Algeria; Morocco; Religion and Politics

Islam has been incorporated in the domestic and foreign policies of government leaders for quite some time (Esposito 1998). However, since the

* I would like to thank Kaltrina Ukmata-Muedini, Matthew Buehler, the editors, and the anonymous reviewers for all of their help and comments. All remaining errors are mine.

Islamic Africa, VOL. 3, NO. 2, 2012. ISSN 2154-0993. www.islamicafricajournal.org

September 11, 2001, terror attacks on the World Trade Center and the Pentagon (Philpott 2002), the teachings of Islam have become a major point of examination. Significant media and policy attention has been directed toward not only understanding Islam, but also discussing how individuals use religion in their political objectives.

And within this discussion is the idea that governments and other actors have aimed to address how to halt the spread of specific Islamic interpretations, in the name of preventing future terror attacks. Because of the worry of particular interpretations of Islam and the effect that they may have on individual actions, many have been quick to try to find other interpretations of Islam (or specific groups of Muslims) to promote. But while such interpretations of Islam have been supported by governments in hopes of preventing future terrorism, Mamdani (2002, 766) argues that within these actions the emphasis by policy-makers has not been on "distinguishing terrorists from civilians," but rather, the "talk has turned religious experience into a political category," and that in order to understand why individuals act, one should not just examine one's religion, nor should religion be viewed in a vacuum (Mamdani 2002). And because of this, a detailed understanding of a range of factors that play a role in an individual's actions is needed. Yet, Mamdani (2002) argues that some are quick to believe that whether one interprets religion itself "literally" compared to "metaphoric or figurative" is the difference in distinguishing whether one will commit acts of terror (767). Applying this specifically to the case of Islam, what he believes is happening is that "we are now told to distinguish between good Muslims and bad Muslims. Mind you, not between good and bad persons, nor between criminals and civil citizens, who both happen to be Muslims, but between good Muslims and bad Muslims" (767).

This last point is important to understand, because with the intention of some to pigeonhole different interpretations of Islam, there has come a move (by some) toward promoting one specific form of Islam, namely Sufism, in the efforts to fight religious extremism. Sufism itself is understood as the mystical branch of Islam (Heck 2007b), although the term "Sufism" is much more complex than just Muslim mysticism[1] (Heck 2007b). And while speaking out against extremism is obviously necessary, within this discussion of attempting to categorize and preempt individuals' actions (and even intentions) based solely on religion, not only has this inaccurately stereotyped Muslims who do not belong to the Sufi teachings of

[1] For a detailed discussion of the term "Sufism," see Heck (2007b).

Islam, but this line of discussion has also led to some suggesting that Sufis themselves are not concerned with politics (and thus are dismissed as any sort of political [violent or nonviolent] challenge to a government).

In fact, this categorization of Sufism as a separate (and non-threatening) entity of Islam has played out recently in the United States with the debate surrounding the construction of the "Park 51 Mosque" in New York City. What is interesting about this case is that here the "good Muslim" was seen as "good" specifically because of an affiliation with Sufism (Safi 2011). Safi (2011) explains that in attempts to show that those individuals who were tied to the creation of the mosque—including Imam Feisal Rauf, the leader of the proposed mosque—were not a threat, news sources, among others, pointed out that he was a Sufi Muslim. The statements by New York leaders such as those of Governor David Patterson fit within this framework of categorizing Islam. Specifically, Safi (2011) quotes Governor Patterson, who when speaking on the mosque construction issue, stated that "this group who has put this mosque together, they are known as the Sufi Muslims. This is not like the Shiites . . . They're almost like a hybrid, almost westernized. They are not really what I would classify in the sort of mainland Muslim practice." By including the "Sufi" in this categorization, this seems to portray the inaccurate picture that Muslim individuals can either be a "Sufi" (and thus the "good" Muslim), or if not a Sufi, an "Islamist" (Safi 2011).

But while this is a recent example of the use of Sufism in politics, this is far from the only case where Sufism has been advocated by governments to counter any potential threat to their political system. In fact, we find evidence where different states have specifically been promoting Sufism, not only because of a positive message that Sufism may provide,[2] but also because Sufism and Sufis are seen as a minimal "political threat" to the current system. This paper will focus primarily on the cases of Algeria and Morocco to illustrate the point of leaders promoting Sufism with the intent to combat not only extremism, but also because of a perception that Sufism is not concerned with politics, and thus not a legitimate political concern to the respective political leaders. However, we are in no way implying that Sufis have only been limited to such a role, as history suggests a far different picture. Many cases exist in which Sufi leaders and groups

[2] It must be noted that even if Sufism does bring a positive message, this does not mean that non-Sufi Muslims, within this false dichotomous framework, do not also offer positive contributions.

have challenged political authority. Furthermore, in many cases, Sufi leaders have had (and continue to have) a great deal of influence compared to political leaders. This paper is merely examining specific cases of where leaders are working under the assumption of "apolitical" Sufis.

Sufism in Politics

As previously alluded to, an underlying belief of Sufism by some has been the idea that Sufis are apolitical, and thus not concerned with either political power, or with those who govern politically. Pinto (2003, 2) explains that "Sufis are usually portrayed as quietest and non-political forces" (citing Gellner 1993, 57–59), "or as simple instruments of state domination" (citing Luizard 1991, 29). But while some may espouse such beliefs toward Sufism and Sufis, the idea of Sufis showing little concern for politics (and only being focused on spiritual matters) is far from accurate (Islam 2002, in Rozehnal 2004; Pinto 2003; Safi 2011). For example, Sufi orders have had a long history of involvement in politics and community affairs (Heck 2007a) that include specific political campaigns against colonialism and authoritarian regimes (Heck 2007a; Pinto 2003, 2). Sufis have also participated in "call[ing] for equality and democracy" (Werbner 1996, 116), and have had a history of political influence in places such as the Sudan (al-Shahi 1979; Collins 2008; Seesemann 2007), Senegal (O'Brian 1975, in Ellis and ter Haar 1998; Clover 2007, in Clark 2009), Morocco (Mojuetan 1981; Zeghal 2009), Lebanon (Hamzeh and Dekmejian 1996), Libya (St. John 2008; Wehrey 2011), and Syria (Weismann 2005). We also find historical examples where political leaders themselves have had connections to Sufi orders (Tarzi 1991). Political leaders have often aimed to establish ties to Sufi leaders (sheikhs) because, as Seesemann (2007) explains, having "good contacts with well-known Sufi leaders may enhance a politician's credibility and give religious legitimacy to his agenda" (32). For this article, the cases of Algeria and Morocco will be used to illustrate how the leaders of these respective states have attempted to promote Sufism in order to combat extremism, but as well to highlight this "apolitical" religious perspective that in turn is seen as a minimal to nonexistent threat to the stability of the leadership currently in power. But while this is the case, it is not the only time that political leaders are approaching Sufism, nor is the use of Sufism limited to just these two states. For example, Seesemann (2007) provides a detailed account of relations between the state and various Sufi groups in Sudan. Specifically in the case of Sudan, the Islamist government attempted to use Sufism and Sufi groups for political gain by working toward dividing the Sufis. Seesemann (2007) explains that

> the distinction between "real" and "false" Sufis is primarily the result of a pragmatic choice guided by political and religious rationalities. In religious terms, al-Turābī's Islamic Movement sees itself as embracing all Muslims, including Sufis qualified as "true" from the Islamist perspective. On the political side, once in power, the Islamist government had to deal with Sufi orders as political lobbies. Here, the Islamists opted for the strategy of courting the "real" Sufis, a strategy that enabled them to achieve two objectives at the same time: 1) the support of several influential Sufi leaders; and 2) a split within the Sufi ranks. (33–34)

What is interesting is that the leadership in Morocco is using what looks to be a similar strategy of dividing different religious groups with the goal of maintaining political strength (Cavatorta 2007).

In another example of the use of Sufism by the state, in the case of Libya, Muammar Qaddafi also appealed to Sufism for specific political goals. Qaddafi, having had a history of attempting to influence religion in Libya (Athanasiadis 2010), for years monitored the activity of religious groups—including Sufis—by controlling funds of Sufi groups, banning Sufi shrines from operating, and limiting the activity of Sufi organizations, because of a belief that they would pose a challenge to his political hold on power (Wehrey 2011). Upon establishing power in 1969, Qaddafi "dissolved the main brotherhoods and persecuted particularly fiercely the Sanussiyah order, which possessed extended charity and economic networks" (Athanasiadis 2010) and was a key organization in anti-colonial efforts against Italy and its colonialism in Libya (Wehrey 2011). However, later a shift occurred in Qaddafi's position on Sufism, where Qaddafi "bolster[ed] Sufi charitable networks as a buffer against radical Salafism" (Wehrey 2011) due to a concern with an increase in Wahhabi interpretations of Islam in Libya. Specifically, some believe that the increase in Libyan fighters in Iraq, as well as the establishment of military training camps in Libya by violent Islamist groups such as the Salafist Group for Preaching and Combat led Qaddafi to advocate Sufi Islam (Athanasiadis 2010). In explaining the increase of attention to Sufism in Libya, Kahlifa Mahdaoui, a military officer, quoted in a 2010 *Global Post* article, says that [Qaddafi] "abolished the *zawāyā* [Sufi prayer halls] but they're now rebuilding them because they realize Wahhabism failed and this is the only way to fight the influence of the U.S. . . . Sufism decreases passions while Wahhabism inflames them."

But while Qaddafi promoted Sufism to counter Islamist groups, he also advocated Sufi thinking toward asceticism in order to challenge what he saw as current actions of "Western colonialism." Qaddafi, speaking on these issues, said:

> Because if we allow ourselves to pursue these and other needs we will be in need of them and their products. We will make ourselves a consumer market. So when Islam calls for Sufism, a rough life and asceticism, it is, in fact, a call which should make us come to our senses and be happy with less, with only the necessary and the good, so that we might be able to do without the many things which are not good for use and which might kill us and gives strength to the enemy . . . Sufism should spread. By Sufism, I do not mean dervishism. Sufism and its modern meaning are not clearly understood in the Islamic world. I do not mean here Sufism as it was portrayed in the old books. For me, Sufism, which is an essence of Islam, should spread . . . In place of the spread of the veil and of preventing women from working, which means treating women with contempt and doubting their ability and their resistance in comparison with men, Sufism and Islamic principles should spread. It should spread instead of the misuse of religion, instead of the jugglery, distortion of religion, Muslim Brotherhood, Takfir Wal-Hijrah . . . and all other calls which have harmed Islam as much as Western Christian colonialism. (BBC 1998)

Algeria

Sufism has had a strong presence in Algeria for centuries. One of the first appearances of Sufism in Algeria was related to Abū Madyan Shu'aib al-Andalusī (Mackeen 1971, 405), who traveled extensively to Morocco, as well as Mecca for religious study, and upon "his return to North Africa he made Bougie the centre of his activity until the year 594/1197, when the reigning Muwahhid sovereign Abū Yūsuf Ya'qūb al-Mansūr (reigned 580–595/1184–1199), disconcerted by the growing popularity of this preacher, ordered his transfer to Marrakesh for trial" (Mackeen 406). The Sufi orders continued to grow extensively after this time, with a number of Sufi orders established throughout North Africa from the sixteenth century onward (Andezian 2002).

One of the larger Algerian Sufi orders, the Tijāniyya Sufi order was established by Ahmed b. Muhammad al-Tijāni (Wright 2005). Al-Tijānī moved to Fez, Morocco, in the year 1799 due to the Ottoman invasion (Benaissa 1997). The Tijāniyya have had (and still have) a large following throughout North Africa (Seesemann 2009). Sufi groups such as the Tijāniyya were a main force against the colonial efforts of France in Algeria. In fact, many Sufi leaders played key roles in the anti-colonialist movement. At the time of French colonialism throughout many parts of the Maghreb, a number of Sufi orders were already in existence (Benaissa 1997). In the earlier nineteenth century, we witnessed one of the first Sufi-led resistance movements by Emir ʻAbd al Qadīr of the Qādiriyya order (Ruedy 2005). In 1834, an agreement was then established between the French government and ʻAbd al Qadīr, giving him control in parts of western Algeria. However, the fighting between these two figures continued, and ʻAbd al Qadīr eventually lost control to France, and was captured in 1847 (Ruedy 1992, 65).

What is interesting to note about this is the way that the French government attempted to use ʻAbd al Qadīr's name for political purposes. As Ruedy (1992) explains,

> throughout the colonial period, the French were at considerable pains to manipulate the legacy of ʻAbd al Qadīr in such a way as to limit its value for Algerian reformers or nationalists. One line of this manipulation focused on what appear to have been the Amir's rather good relations with the French after he left for the Near East: his friendship with Napoleon III, the contention that the resistance leader in his later years believed the French occupation to be beneficial for Algeria, and in particular the claim that he condemned the massive Kabylie insurrection of 1871. (65)

But even after ʻAbd al Qadīr, the Sufi resistance to French colonialism continued into the late nineteenth and twentieth centuries. Benaissa (1997) cites Sufi sheikhs whose emphasis during colonialism was to increase the faith and "piety" of citizens, as this was seen as one aspect of anti-colonial resistance. Benaissa (1997) explains that "this piety . . . was the best form of the [defense] against the more insidious, because less visible, forces of the secularization that underlay the French *mission civilitrice;* colonialism as stressed at the outset, was not just an assault on external liberty, it was, much more, an attack on the traditional Muslim mentality and way of life."

However, not all Sufis were opposed to French activities in Algeria.

For example, some within the Tijāniyya order continued to maintain a relationship with political leaders of the state, and in the case of the twentieth century in Algeria, with the French colonial power (Seesemann and Soares 2009). For example, Seesemann and Soares (2009) explain that France attempted to shore up support from Muslims in their colonies during both World War I and World War II, with a goal of establishing backing from Sufi leaders during these periods of time (94–95). One major Sufi leader who had a close relationship with the French government was Sidi Benamor, a leading figure in the Tijāniyya order. The French government, aware of "Sidi Benamor's known pro-French proclivities" (Seesemann and Soares 2009, 98), allowed him to travel to other areas of North Africa to meet with fellow Tijāni Sufis. They backed this trip because of a belief that having ties to Sidi Benamor would help in terms of continuing their work as a colonial power in areas of heavy resistance. Seesemann and Soares (2009) go on to explain that "Sidi Benamor seems to have been traveling on a semiofficial mission, at least in French colonies" (99). Thus, this trip benefited France since some speeches given by Sidi Benamor were quite supportive of French actions, and ran counter to many of the anti-colonialist movements (Seesemann and Soares 2009).

Following colonialism, the Sufis were mostly pushed out of any control of power due to the Salafi influence in Algeria (Andezian 2002). But while Sufi leaders may have had limited direct access to national governance, Sufi orders were still prevalent in Algeria, continuing to function as religious institutions (Andezian 2002). Fauque (1961) (in Trimingham 1971, 256) reported that the Khalwatiyya, the Shādhiliyya, and the Qādiriyya orders combined had a total of 500,000 adherents, whereas other figures suggest that right before independence (in 1961), it was believed that four of the larger Sufi groups (Khalwatiyya, Shādhiliyya, Qādiriyya, and Khalwatiyya) had roughly 500,000 members (Benaissa 1997). However, we saw that it was after Boumediene when Sufi orders had more room to operate; some who were previously seen as a challenge to the government now had more freedoms within the state (Andezian 2002).

Islamism, Sufism, and the Algerian State

In Algeria, the government has historically experienced violent confrontations with Islamist organizations. The rise of the Islamist groups intensified in the 1980s with a range of protests in Algiers and other areas within Algeria related to what was seen as ineffective economic policies, as well as Chadli Bendjedid and his government's inability to address the political concerns of citizens. In 1989, after Bendjedid adopted a new constitution that allowed for new political parties to form, the Islamic Salvation Front (FIS) decided to enter the electoral political system. In the 1990 local elections, the rules for the elections stated that if no party won a majority, the party with the most votes would gain the majority of seats. And although it became obvious that the electoral rules "[were] clearly designed to favor the largest party which all presumed to be the FLN [National Liberation Front]" (Ruedy 2005, 253), the FIS came away victorious, successfully winning a majority of seats (Ruedy 2005).

In response to this, the government had a number of FIS leaders arrested. In addition, to counter any potential victory, the state redrew electoral districts, and limited where the Islamists could campaign. Nevertheless, in the first part of the 1992 elections, "the FIS won absolute majorities in 188 of the 430 electoral districts" (Ruedy 2005, 255). Because of the overall expected FIS victory, military leaders put pressure on Chadli Bendjedid to resign, formed the High State Council (HCE), and banned the FIS as a political party. In response, the FIS and police both engaged in acts of violence where thousands of individuals, including many innocent bystanders, were killed. The total number of those killed in the civil conflict between the government, FIS, and other Islamist groups is said to be as high as 150,000 persons (Ruedy 2005).

It is from this historical context that we should examine the use of Sufism as related to government domestic policy. Specifically, due to the prolonged conflict with Islamists in Algeria, "since the early nineties of the last century, the authorities have found a different way of stemming the influence of the Salafi jihadist ideology which is espoused by the armed hardliners" (BBC 2009). The government has attempted to highlight Sufism to counter any interpretation of Salafi Islam that has been seen as problematic to the state (Al Jazeera 2008). Algerian President Abdul Aziz Bouteflika specifically has emphasized the spread of Sufism as a counter to Al Qaeda (*World Tribune* 2009), and the government has taken a number of steps to promote Sufism as an attempt to counter extremist ideologies. For example, Francois Burgat (2003) explains that

> in 1990 and 1991, a number of analysts tried to pretend that the old guard of the Algerian [*Zāwiyas*], who had been erased from national history because of their alleged collaboration with the colonial authorities, would save the country from the growing threat of the FIS. From a Sufist perspective, the

> Islamists are regularly described as "foreign," excluding themselves from a "political system based on Sunni principles," which is itself a continuation of "Ottoman influence." The fact that brotherhoods would often ignore national boundaries is often conveniently forgotten, so that a "good," "endogenous" Sufism is promoted, as opposed to an imported Islamism. (66)

Burgat (2003) goes on to explain how Sufism was seen as the "good" Islam in Algeria due to the belief that Sufis had a political loyalty to the state compared to Islamists who were counter to the state authorities by saying:

> For Algeria, the picture of "good" Maliki Sufis, and "good" North Africans threatened by the bearded Wahhabis from faraway Arabia, is passed off as scientific observation. This type of political skullduggery is not always condemned. The author of a study on the (good) "religion of the people" was happy to note that "if such an amount of information and facts about the Algerian [*Zāwiyas*] had been made available to the general public over a period of not more than three months (May to July 1991), it was only due to the 'democratic wind' that was beginning to sweep the country." The [*Zāwiyas'*] progra[m] seemed, unsurprisingly, to consist of "pledging allegiance to the President of the Republic" and "confronting anyone who, in the name of Wahhabism, or Shiism, or of any other imported rite, has attempted and is attempting to tamper with the Maliki rite, held in common by most of our population." (66)

More recently, Bouteflika has attempted to use the mosques in regard to Islam, and has also looked to the help of Sufi groups such as the Tijāniyya for support (Porter 2008). Porter (2008) argues that

> Algiers augments its projection of hard power with a comprehensive soft power campaign. In particular, it is building a large mosque complex on Tamanrasset's highest point. The mosque succinctly conveys the state's intention to exercise influence, if not outright control, over Islamic activity in the city. Beyond the mosque, the state also promotes the activities of Sufi religious orders. These orders have historically been powerful in the region and the Tijāniyya in particular has proven to be a valuable supporter of Bouteflika's National Liberation Front (FLN). (15)

In 2006 Abdelaziz Belkadem, the prime minister of Algeria, spoke at a colloquium held by the Tijāniyya order, saying that "he wanted to use this meeting and the [*zaouias*] (religious centre) both as a centre of influence and as platforms from which the precepts of our religion can be propagated" (Aflou 2006). Along with the comments by the prime minister, Abdelaziz Bouteflika also sent a message, part of which was a call to "emphasize the spiritual, human and aesthetic values of Islam when we explain it to non-Muslims and show them the true nature of this great religion" (Aflou 2006).

Along the lines of past approaches by leaders emphasizing Sufism against political Islamist groups because of a belief that the Sufis would be a counterforce to Islamism—and loyal adherents to government authority—the Algerian government more recently has continued to operate under this assumption of Sufism as a possible ally. For example, "the authorities have created a television and radio station to promote Sufism and the [*zawais*] or religious confraternities that preach and practi[c]e it, in addition to regular appearances by Sufi sheiks on the stations" (Chikhi 2009). The government has taken this approach after an increase in violent conflict with the Islamist groups who have challenged the government. In fact, the government has actually suggested that the *zawāyā* increase their level of involvement in civil society by providing various social services (Chikhi 2009). An Algerian sheikh by the name of Belabes Lazhari was quoted in a report (Ramzi, Ali, Arfaoui, and Wedoud 2010) as saying that "the current wager rests on the ability of Sufis to give expression to Islam and present it in a sound manner, and the extent of their contribution to cultural exchanges and renouncing violence, extremism and terrorism."

In July 2010, the BBC (2009) reported that the government of Algeria has specifically organized events that highlight the message of Sufism. This specific event brought together over 5,000 persons to participate in "lectures and seminars calling for moderation and shunning hard-line behavi[or]." In addition, "the Islamic Affairs Ministry was also prepared to allow Sufis to distribute literature, CDs and books to schools and mosques. Officials said the Sufis were expecting to appeal to young Muslims" (*World Tribune* 2009). The aim was to increase the message of respect for others, ideas that are found in Islam (BBC 2009). The government believes that these actions will appeal to the youth in Algeria (*World Tribune* 2009).

Morocco

Examining the political and religious history of Morocco, we also find strong Sufi influences in the realm of politics, in terms of both Sufi saints

(Cornell 1998, 114–15) and Sufi orders. Sufism seemed to first be present in Morocco in "the beginning of the eleventh century" (Cornell 1998, 4), but continued to expand. Throughout the centuries Sufi orders were very much involved in religious, political, and economic issues, at times becoming major threats to other religious and political leaders. For example, Sufi orders in Morocco such as the Nāsiriyya and Dilā'iyya served a critical role in local trade issues in Morocco in the seventeenth to nineteenth centuries. The level of Sufi influence was a major issue for the ruling political leaders. As Gutelius (2002) explains, the Sufis

> . . . challenged the legitimacy of the emerging 'Alawi family as the true leaders of the faithful, to which 'Alawi leaders responded with force. In 1668, Sultan Mulay Rashid forced the leaders of the Dilā'iyya into exile in Fez and destroyed the *zāwiya* of Sīdī Ahmed ū Mūsā in 1670, the center of one of the most powerful religious families south of the Atlas mountains. He also repeatedly threatened the Nāsiriyya, though he did not live long enough to carry out these threats. (31)

However, state leaders well before this time not only took notice of Sufi influence, but also "courted urban and rural [S]ufi orders, hoping to gain their allegiance to an otherwise politically fragmented state, and they relied on populist Sufi movements in organizing jihads against the Portuguese" (Gutelius 2002, 31). And while it was not always the case that Sufis were involved in such activities,[3] many orders were involved in politics (Gutelius 2002).

In the case of the Nāsiriyya, the order was popular for spiritual reasons, as well as for the economic benefits that the order could deliver for individuals. For example, as the order expanded, they had connections to "credit and to its property holdings, including land, water resources, [and] *zawāyā* and granaries" (Gutelius 2002, 32). This economic influence elevated to a point where such leaders were "mediators" (Gutelius 2002, 33) for the society. Nāsiri leaders also aided individuals in trade. For example, they would often collect a tax called the "zattāt (passage toll or protection toll)" (Gutelius 2002, 34) that would be used to help the traders make it to their

[3] For example, in the mid- to late seventeenth century, the Nāsiriyya order "gained a reputation for remaining aloof from the struggles of temporal authorities over the throne—a position that attracted many followers and allied, and helped to protect the order from makhzan persecution" (Gutelius 2002, 31).

destination without issue. And because of that influence, the Nāsiri leaders aimed to establish political clout within the broader community. However, "this political influence spread far beyond local affairs . . . The 'Alawi sultans themselves occasionally relied on Nāsiri leaders to solve political difficulties and recognized the order's wide appeal" (Gutelius 2002, 38–39). For this reason, many members of the government made sure that the Sufi leaders were not bothered. It must be noted, however, that the role of the Nāsiri Sufi order was not always as influential politically as it was in the later seventeenth century and early eighteenth century. The reason for this is that during the mid-eighteenth century, Morocco began to increase trade with outside actors, and this had an effect on the Nāsiriyya. New agreements with Europe, as well as increased roles by a whole host of other Sufi orders (such as "the Darqāwiyya, the Wazzāniyya, the Kunta-led Qādiriyya and the Tijāniyya"), altered the role of the Nāsiriyya (Gutelius 2002, 40).

In the nineteenth and twentieth centuries, an influence of Salafi and Wahhabi Islam began to take hold in Morocco, much of which was often at the expense of Sufi orders, with many Wahhabi leaders looking to have the government move away from the *shirk* or "polytheism" of Sufism as they saw it (Zeghal 2008, 17). This attitude toward Sufi orders was taken up by leaders such as Mawlay Sulaymān who

> denounced aspects of the conduct of some brotherhoods but did not reject Sufism in principle. The doctrine turned out to be politically useful to him because it enabled him to criticize the brotherhoods threatening his authority, such as the Sharqawiyya and the Tayyibiyya—allied to Berber tribes that the [*Makhzen*] could not control—and the Darqawiyya, which represented a real challenge to the Sultan. (Zeghal 2008, 17)

Salafi Islam began to influence leaders' decisions about Islam, which ultimately affected the treatment of Sufi orders (Zeghal 2008, 18).[4]

But while Salafi beliefs gained support among many religious and political leaders, many Sufi orders still existed in Morocco from 1900 onward (Geertz 1979, 155). In fact, Sufi orders not only continued to exist, but also maintained a presence in the political sphere of society, often challenging colonialism, as well as the domestic political leaders. For

---

[4] What is interesting, however, is that a number of former political leaders, after being removed from office, would often join a Sufi order (Zeghal 2008, 18).

example, Sufi sheikh Muhammad bin ʻAbd al-Kabīr al-Kattānī was a major challenge to not only French colonialism, but also to the sultan (Bazzaz 2010). Because of his position against the Moroccan leadership—who were threatened by his influence—al-Kattānī was accused of heresy in 1896, and in the year 1909 was arrested, and eventually died under custody. In addition, the sultan also went after the Kattāniyya order that remained (Bazzaz 2010). One reason why al-Kattānī and the Kattāniyya order were seen as a major challenge to the political authority in Morocco was because they said they were "descendants of Muhammad" (Bazzaz 2010, 11), "which the Khattāniyya leadership deployed to articulate its sense of political legitimacy in its efforts to reassert the leadership role of *shurafa* lineage" (Bazzaz 2010, 11).

However, it would be incorrect to suggest that the Moroccan political leadership, the "*makhzan,*" always took such a contrary approach with al-Kattānī. In fact, at one point, they attempted to establish an "alliance" with al-Kattānī (Bazzaz 2010, 66). Bazzaz (2010) explains that "from the state's perspective, an alliance with the shaykh of an active and expanding Sufi movement held many possibilities. By drawing on Muhammad al-Kattānī's gaining spiritual and social authority among the people in Fez, the *makhzan* stood to bolster its waning legitimacy there" (66). This ultimately affected the *makhzan*'s influence negatively, with al-Kattānī gaining further support by many in Morocco (Bazzaz 2010).

Sufi groups continued to be influential in various aspects of Moroccan society throughout the twentieth century, not only in terms of religious issues, but in the economic sectors as well (Geertz 1979). For example, Sufi *zawāyā* were key in terms of serving a political (Bazzaz 2010) and economic role in relation to local trade in Morocco, with significant influence in the marketplace (Geertz 1979). But along with this major presence in the markets, the *zawāyā* were also influential in politics. For example, the *zawāyā* were involved in a number of political actions during French colonialism (Geertz 1979). They began to lose power, however, with the rise of the Istiqlal party, which saw itself as "opposed to the existing zawias" (Geertz 1979, 162–63). In fact, the post-independence leaders of Morocco wanted "simultaneously to divide its representatives to weaken them and also gather them around the throne to control them" (Zeghal 2009, 31). They aimed to dictate and monitor religious action by controlling funding in many cases, or the supervision of the *zawāyā.* They also attempted to monitor religious activity by placing the Ministry of Religious Affairs under the watch of the top leaders (Zeghal 2009).

Islamism, Sufism, and the Moroccan State

Similar to Algeria, governments in Morocco have had an interest in establishing control over religion. As mentioned, this was evident during the early years after independence (Zeghal 2009), as well as in later decades, which can be seen when examining the threat of political Islam to the monarchy and the different responses taken by the government to this threat. For example, government interest in the control of religion was quite evident under Hassan II, who came to power in 1961. In an attempt to gain religious legitimacy, Hassan II stipulated in the constitution that the leader of the state would be seen as the "commander of the faithful" (Zeghal 2009, 44). Hassan II also showed interest in attempting to speak on matters of religion (Zeghal 2009). But while the government had a strong control over religion in Morocco, the presence of Islamists was not completely absent (Howe 2005). For example, Hassan II continued to enforce his commitment to Islam through the support of Islamic family law, which showed the influence of non-governmental religious groups (Howe 2005).

But despite this earlier influence, Islamists generally took a back seat to secular and modernization policies up until the 1980s. Historically, Islamist groups in Morocco became more active during Nasser's reign in Egypt, and in attempts to counter Gamal Abdel Nasser's policy of socialism, the Moroccan government of Hassan II allowed Islamists to operate, with the help of the Saudi Arabian government (Howe 2005), which funded these groups. However, "by the mid-1980s, the palace had realized that Islamic radicals were a potential threat. King Hassan openly encouraged so-called moderate Islamists, that is, those who recognized his authority as Commander of the Faithful, and tightened controls on the others" (Howe 2005, 126). Similar threats by both extremist and also nonviolent Islamists continued into the 1990s with the establishment of the Justice and Development Party (PJD) in 1997. The PJD, with its emphasis on nonviolence and claims to want to "work within the system" (Howe 2005, 134), as well as their goal of establishing shari'ah or Islamic law as a political system of Morocco, was seen as a challenge to Hassan II (Howe 2005). This concern intensified when the PJD, running in less than the full list of districts, managed to place third in the 2002 elections.

But while the PJD posed a nonviolent threat to Mohammed VI—who in 1999 took power after the death of his father Hassan II—violent Islamist groups were also active at this time in Morocco. In 2002, individuals with ties to Al Qaeda were found to be operating in the Moroccan city of

Casablanca (Howe 2005). On May 16, 2003, Morocco experienced a major terror attack "in which 14 suicide bombers identified as Salafiya Jihadiya adherents linked to the Moroccan Islamic Combatant Group (GICM) and Al Qaeda attacked five Western and Jewish targets in Casablanca, killing 45 and injuring more than 100" (Migdalovitz 2010, 2). Another terror attack was carried out "in April 2007, [when] two suicide attacks occurred near the U.S. Consulate and the American Language Center in Casablanca; the bombers killed only themselves" (Migdalovitz 2010, 3).

In response to these attacks, Mohammed VI went after terror organizations in Morocco, and has shared information with other states about terror groups in an attempt to halt their activities (Migdalovitz 2010). In addition to this, Mohammed VI has also taken a number of steps to influence the role of religion in Morocco. Migdalovitz (2010) explains that

> to counter radical Islamism, Morocco also has exerted greater control over religious leaders and councils, created new theological councils, retrained imams, deployed supervisors to oversee their sermons, closed unregulated mosques, retrained and rehabilitated some individuals convicted of terror-related crimes to correct their understanding of Islam, and launched radio and television stations and a website to transmit "Moroccan religious values" of tolerance. In 2005, the king launched a $1.2 billion National Initiative for Human Development to redress socioeconomic conditions extremists exploit for recruitment. (3)

It is within this approach that we see that Mohammed VI has been attempting to use Sufism within his domestic policy to counter Islamist groups (and specifically Salafi Islam) (Al Jazeera 2009), although the level of "success" in such policies is unclear (Mostapha El Khalifi, in Al Jazeera 2009). Specifically, because the attacks were "perpetrated by Jihadist groups inspired by the literalist interpretations of Salafi Islam, the Moroccan regime closed dozens of Quranic schools that were believed to be the cent[er]s of Salafist preaching and pushed to kindle public interest in Sufism" (Habboush 2009). The Moroccan government has found an interest in using Sufism in its domestic religious policies because of what it sees as Sufism's "flexibility, clearly in comparison here with the rigidity of radical forms of religious interpretations" (Maghraoui 2009, 206). In fact, even some Sufis themselves blame the increase in Islamic extremism in Morocco on the fact that Sufism has not played a larger role in society (Habboush 2009).

What is interesting about this policy approach is that the Moroccan government has not been consistent on its position toward religion, as it has advocated the role of the mosque, while at the same time establishing other policies that are seen as being against religion (El Khalifi, in Al Jazeera 2009). In discussing the use of Sufism in Morocco before and after the September 11, 2001, terror attacks, Mohammad Zarif (Al Jazeera 2008) explains that "the significance of Sufism is determined by the nature of religious activists. This means that before the September 11 attacks in 2001, Sufism had a limited role to play . . . But after September 11, the state became aware of the danger of the Salafi movement and started to make use of Sufism to create the desired balance." In terms of his support for Sufism, Mohammed VI has specifically "brought together local Sufi leaders [in Morocco] and offered millions of dollars in aid to use as a bulwark against radical fundamentalism (*U.S. News and World Report* 2005).

One of the main Sufi orders that Mohammed VI has worked with has been the Bushishiyya order. The Bushishiyya, which came out of the Qādiriyya order (Zeghal 2009), was "first established among the Berber tribes of the Beni Snassen Maasif (Northeast Morocco) in about 1942 by Abū Madyan ib Munawar al-Budshish" (Sedwick 2004, 133). The order's numbers have risen since the 1960s, with overall membership said to be at around 15,000 persons (Zeghal 2009, 89). In addition, the Bushishiyya are said to be increasing membership among "elites" in Morocco (Sedwick 2004). In terms of Mohammed VI reaching out to the Bushishiyya Sufi order, Mohamed Zarif, in an interview with Al Jazeera (2008), explains that

> in 2002, the government appointed a member of the Buchachiya order—the strongest Sufi order in the country[,] as the minister in charge of Islamic endowments. More importantly, before 2002, we used to say that Morocco's Islamic identity was made up of two components: the Ash'ari creed and the Maliki Islamic doctrine. But since 2002, a third component has been added to our Islamic identity, that is, Sunni Sufism of [the] Al-Junaid al-Salik order. Thus Sufism has become an integral part of the religious identity . . . (Al Jazeera, 2008)

Sedwick (2004) explains that one key point about Bushishiyya Sufism is that one doesn't see "the function of the *shaykh* as patron and intermediary in political and economic affairs (though it remains to be seen how well this will resist the pressures created by increasing Bushishi presence in government)" (139). This allows political leaders to continue to have their authority unchallenged by Sufi leaders.

Along with the support of the Bushishi in the context of a state position, Mohammed VI has also taken other steps to promote Sufism. For example, the government has supported a number of different Sufi music events. In addition, different Sufi festivals have brought together a host of academics and performers "around a variety of themes such as Sufism, human rights, intercultural dialogue, religious tolerance and human development" (Maghraoui 2009, 207). In 2009, Mohammed VI organized a Sufi conference entitled the "Second World Sidi Chiker Gathering" (Sidi Chiker 2011) in Marrakech, Morocco, which over 1,000 Sufi Muslims attended. Here, Mohammed VI wrote a letter that emphasized the historical relationship between the Moroccan leaders and Sufi sheikhs. In his remarks, read at the event (by the "Moroccan Minister of Religious Affairs" [Sidi Chiker 2011]), Mohammed VI stated that

> You are all aware of the symbolic relationship which has always existed between Imarate Al Muminin (Commandership of the Faithful) in this nation and the chief Sufi leaders. They have endeav[or]ed together to preserve the country's Sunni creed and its doctrinal orientations. (Sidi Chiker, 2011)

In Mohammed VI's letter, he continued to reiterate the importance of Sufism in regards to issues in Morocco, specifically stating that "in addition to their ability to identify the roots of the problem and propose solutions, . . . the great perspicacity of the Sufis has helped them to identify a way forwards whenever the interests of our community have been at stake" (Touahri 2009). In addition, Mohammed VI has funded various Sufi *zawāyā* in order to continue the visibility of this approach in Islam (al-Ashraf 2010). Sufism has been given a spotlight in Morocco, where the government has helped highlight Sufi groups' ability to teach others about their beliefs (al-Ashraf 2010). The idea behind this promotion of Sufism is that Sufi "teaching can provide a remedy for problems currently faced by states, such as terrorism and extremism" (Touahri 2009).

But while this idea of promoting Sufism has been partly used to counter violent extremism, the reason for this approach does not seem to be limited to just countering violent extremism. This seems to be the case because Mohammed VI has used Sufism to counter challenging political parties such as the Islamist Justice and Development Party (PJD) (al-Ashraf 2010), which is seen as "a major political force" (McFaul and Wittes 2008, 22), and the biggest political threat to Mohammed VI's regime. In fact, "Islamist parties and organizations [operating within the political system] pose the most serious challenge to the king's power. They could inject a new dynamic into Moroccan politics, possibly leading to political reform" (Ottaway and Riley 2006, 14). The PJD has gained in popularity by running on an anti-corruption platform, all the while being an active provider of a range of social services in the state (McFaul and Wittes 2008).[5]

Sufism has therefore been used as a critical tool by the Moroccan government because the leadership seems to want individuals to practice a religion that does not emphasize becoming involved in the political system, and their belief seems to suggest that Sufism falls under this structure of not emphasizing political action (Al Jazeera 2008). For example, in a 2008 speech that Mohammed VI gave to the Sidi Chiker National Gathering of Sufi Partisans (Maghreb Arab Presse, 2008), he seemed to advocate the message of Sufism refraining from politics by saying:

> Although mysticism is mostly about communion and spiritual refinement, it also impacts society in several ways; for example, through acts of solidarity, mutual assistance, by wanting good things for others, through forgiveness and tolerance, and by addressing the minds and the hearts to cleanse them. It is important to stress, in this respect, that Sufi [*zāwiyas*] should seek to remain true to the concept of purity upon which they are based. They should forgo earthly pursuits. Sufi disciples should steer away from acts and attitudes which do not become them, give up any quest for worldly rewards and, instead, seek higher, loftier goals. (Magreb Arab Presse, 2008)

[5] Secular parties in the past have joined to support Mohammed VI in order to counter any Islamist challenge, and some suggest that such parties could either side with the Islamists against the king, or become part of the government, thus gaining some political power, but at the expense of advancing a democratic system against the political repression of the king (Ottaway and Riley 2006). This has helped the PJD, as it was not seen as being aligned with the undemocratic leadership of Mohammed VI (McFaul and Wittes 2008).

He highlights the importance of Sufism to Moroccan culture by further saying:

> As for service to the nation, it is accomplished through the observance of your duties and obligations towards the ultimate Imamate, namely the Commandership of the Faithful, and the keen desire to preserve the cultural specificities of Morocco and protect them against alien trends and influences. (Magreb Arab Presse, 2008)

Dr. Abbas Boughanem, in an interview with Al-Arabiya, emphasizes this idea that Mohammed VI has promoted the idea of Sufism not just to combat religious extremism, but also because of the belief that Sufis will teach others "who follow them some kind of political passisity" (al-Ashraf 2010). Maghraoui (2009) explains this duel use of Sufism in Morocco when he explains that

> through the organization of the famous Fez spiritual festival as well as through special TV and radio [programs], Sufism is now experiencing a significant revival in the Moroccan public sphere as part of a religiosity that encourages interfaith dialogue, universalism, tolerance, love, peace, harmony through a language that is effectively depoliticized. (206)

What is important to note, however, is that in the promotion of Sufism, the government is attempting to "divide" the religious groups in Morocco (Cavatorta 2007). In fact, the king has been able to pin two major Sufi-influenced religious groups—Jamait al-Adl and the Bushishiyya order—against one another. Cavatorta (2007) explains that because of not only the popularity of Jamait al-Adl (led by Shaykh Abdelsalam Yassine), but also due to their strong protest against the political system within Morocco,

> the monarchy entertains privileged relations with the *Tarīqa* and its leaders. This alliance is possible because the *Tarīqa* does not challenge the *imarat al mouminine* and does not believe that the association should be directly engaged in politics, but should instead only be concerned with the betterment of the individual members. The King therefore supports the *Tarīqa* in order to strengthen his religious legitimacy and to have privileged access to the religious bourgeoisie that the association represents. In exchange, the *Tarīqa* enjoys freedom from scrutiny and, occasionally, obtains political [favors] like the royal appointment of the

leader's son to the post of governor of the Berkane province. (Jamai 2005, in Cavatorta 2007).

Conclusion

This essay has examined the use of Sufi Islam by the North African governments of Algeria and Morocco in attempts to challenge other interpretations of Islam. We have shown that one main reason why governments seem to have promoted Sufism is not solely to appreciate what Sufism has to offer as a religious approach, but rather because with the promotion of Sufism, some suggest that those who follow Sufism will have little concern for politics, thus possibly reducing the political threat to the state, despite evidence to suggest that Sufis in the history of Algeria have been involved in politics. Furthermore, evidence of Sufi involvement in politics is still taking place today.

We find that in the cases of Algeria and Morocco leaders have promoted Sufism through state-sponsored programs such as support for religious buildings, as well as showing their support by allowing Sufis to be active with conferences, and also allowing Sufis the ability to distribute information. In addition, we find that some of the most challenging political opponents to the regimes in Algeria and Morocco are Islamist parties. Thus, the governments seem to use Sufism in attempts to influence individuals on Islam, while aiming to challenge other Islamist organizations. Future research will explore how other leaders of both Muslim and non-Muslim majority states aim to promote Sufism as a counter to Islamist movements, as this approach is not limited to just a few cases.

This article does not suggest that one cannot highlight Sufi contributions in society. In fact, studies have looked at Sufi approaches to international affairs, setting the discussion within the tradition of Islam, and how Sufism, for example, can offer *another* perspective into Muslim arguments of global justice (Said and Funk 2001; 2004) and human rights (Muedini 2010). But this in no way means that Sufism is the only approach from within Islam that offers such ideas. This is far from the case. But to suggest that religion itself is the sole variable in predicting one's beliefs and actions is problematic. Namely, attempts to understand one's level of political involvement cannot be understood by solely reducing explanations to one's type of religious affiliation; political interests and positions (or the lack thereof) should not be divorced from socioeconomic issues, as well as historical and political contexts.

References

Aflou, L. 2006. "The Tidjani Brotherhood—The Other Face of Islam." *Magharebia,* November 27, 2006. Available online: http://www.magharebia.com/cocoon/awi/xhtml1/en_GB/features/awi/features/2006/11/27/feature-01.

Al-Ashraf. 2010. "Government Organizes Sufi Seminars and Festivals: Morocco Fights Islamist Extremism with Sufism." *Al Arabiya.* Available online: http://www.alarabiya.net/articles/2010/09/26/120366.html.

Al Jazeera. 2008. "Promoting Sufism Is Strategy to Fight Extremism in Morocco, Algeria, Experts Say." November 28, 2008. Transcript. BBC Worldwide Monitoring.

———. 2009. "Morocco: Religious Revival on the Rise Among Youths, Study Says." October 5, 2009. Transcript. BBC Worldwide Monitoring.

Al-Shahi, A. 1979. "Traditional Politics and a One-Party System in Northern Sudan." *Bulletin (British Society for Middle Eastern Studies)* 6, no. 1, pp. 3–12.

Andezian, S. 2002. "The Significance of Sufism in Algeria in the Aftermath of Independence." *Religious Studies Unit* 2002, PASSIA. Thursday, December 12. Available online: http://www.passia.org/meetings/rsunit/2002/Sufism-minutes3.htm.

Athanasiadis, I. 2010. "Libya's Islamic Reform Model." *Global Post.* May 2010. Available online: http://www.globalpost.com/dispatch/middle-east/100210/libya-gadhafi-sufi-islam?page=0,1.

Bazzaz, S. 2010. *Forgotten Saints: History, Power, and Politics in the Making of Modern Morocco.* Cambridge, Mass.: Harvard University Press.

BBC. 1998. "Libya Qadhafi Addresses Students of Islam: Calls for Muslim Unity in Face of 'Western Colonialism.'" August 24, 1998. BBC Summary of World Broadcasts. Text of speech made by Col. Qadhafi in Tripoli on August 18, Tripoli television 2010 on August 21, 1988.

———. 2009. "Algeria Said Using Sufism to Stem Propagation of Salafi Jihadist Ideology." July 27, 2009.

Benaissa, O. 1997. "Algerian Sufism in the Colonial Period." In *Algeria, Revolution Revisited*, ed. Reza Shah-Kazemi, 47–68. London: Islamic World Report. Available online: http://majlis-al-uns.over-blog.com/article-algerian-sufism-in-the-colonial-period-82985688.html.

Burgat, F. 2003. *Face to Face with Political Islam.* London: I. B. Tauris.

Cavatorta, F. 2007. "More Than Repression: The Significance of *Divide et Impera* in the Middle East and North Africa: The Case of Morocco." *Journal of Contemporary African Studies* 25, no. 2, pp. 187–203.

Chikhi, Lamine. 2009. "Algeria Sponsors Sufism to Fight Extremism." Reuters. Accessed on February 3, 2010. Available online: http://uk.reuters.com/article/2009/07/08/algeria-islam-violence-idUKL721135820090708.

Clark, A. 2009. Review of *Sufism and Jihad in Modern Senegal: The Murid Order,* by John Glover. *American Historical Review* 114, no. 4, pp. 1198–99.

Collins, R. 2008. *A History of Modern Sudan.* Cambridge, Eng.: Cambridge University Press.

Cornell, V. J. 1998. *Realm of the Saint: Power and Authority in Moroccan Sufism.* Austin: University of Texas Press.

Ellis, S., and G. ter Haar. 1998. "Religion and Politics in Sub-Saharan Africa." *Journal of Modern African Studies* 36, no. 2, pp. 175–201.

Esposito, J. 1998. *Islam and Politics.* Syracuse, N.Y.: Syracuse University Press.

Fauque, L. P. 1961. "Ou en est l'Islam traditionnel en Algeria?" *L'Afrique et l'Asie*, no. 55, pp. 17–22.

Geertz, C. 1979. "Suq: The Bazaar Economy in Sefrou." In *Meaning and Order in Moroccan Society: Three Essays in Cultural Analysis,* ed. Clifford Geertz, Hildred Geertz, and Lawrence Rosen. Cambridge, Eng.: Cambridge University Press.

Gellner, E. 2003. *Muslim Society.* Cambridge, Eng.: Cambridge University Press.

Glover, J. 2007. *Sufism and Jihad in Modern Senegal: The Murid Order.* Rochester, N.Y.: Rochester University Press.

Gutelius, D. V. 2002. "The Path Is Easy and the Benefits Large: The Nāsiriyya, Social Networks and Economic Change in Morocco, 1640–1830." *Journal of African History* 43, no. 1, pp. 27–49.

Habboush, M. 2009. "Moroccan Youth Rediscover Sufi Heritage." *The National.* September 19, 2009. Available online: http://www.thenational.ae/news/worldwide/middle-east/moroccan-youth-rediscover-sufi-heritage?pageCount=0.

Hamzeh, A. N., and H. Dekmejian. 1996. "A Sufi Response to Political Islamism: Al-Ahbash of Lebanon." *International Journal of Middle East Studies* 28, no. 2, pp. 217–29.

Heck, P., ed. 2007a. *Sufism and Politics: The Power of Spirituality.* Princeton, N.J.: Markus Weiner.

———. 2007b. "Sufism—What Is It Exactly?" *Religion Compass* 1, no. 1, pp. 148–64.

———. 2010. "The Politics of Sufism: Is There One?" In *Sufism Today: Heritage and Tradition in the Global Community*, ed. Catharina Raudvere and Leif Sternberg, pp. 13–29.

Howe, M. 2005. *Morocco: The Islamist Awakening and Other Challenges*. New York: Oxford University Press.

Jamai, A. 2005. "Quand la Boutchichiya fait de la politique." *Le Journal Hebdomadaire*, February 3.

Luizad, P. J. 1991. "Le role des confreries Soufies dans le systeme politique egyptien." In *Monde Arabe Maghreb,* Machrek 131 (January/March), pp. 26–53.

Mackeen, A. M. M. 1971. "The Early History of Sufism in the Maghrib Prior to Al-Shadhili (d. 656/1258)." *Journal of the American Oriental Society* 91, no. 3, pp. 398–408.

Maghraoui, D. 2009. "The Strengths and Limits of Religious Reforms in Morocco." *Mediterranean Politics* 14, no. 2, pp. 195–211.

Maghreb Arab Presse. 2008. "Full Text of King's Message to 1st Sidi Chiker National Gatherings of Sufi Partisans." Available online: http://www.map.ma/eng/sections/speeches/full_text_of_king_s9461/view.

Mamdani, M. 2002. "Good Muslim, Bad Muslim: A Political Perspective on Culture and Terrorism." *American Anthropologist* 104, no. 3, pp. 766–75.

McFaul, M., and T. C. Wittes. 2008. "The Limits of Limited Reforms." *Journal of Democracy* 19, no. 1, pp. 19–33.

Migdalovitz, C. 2010. "Morocco: Current Issues." Congressional Research Service. December 20, 2010. Available online: http://www.fas.org/sgp/crs/row/RS21579.pdf.

Mojuetan, B. A. 1981. "Legitimacy in a Power State: Moroccan Politics in the Seventeenth Century During the Interregnum." *International Journal of Middle East Studies* 13, no. 3, pp. 347–60.

Muedini, F. 2010. "Examining Islam and Human Rights from the Perspective of Sufism." *Muslim World Journal of Human Rights* 7, no. 1, pp. 1–23.

O'Brien, D. B. C. 1975. *Saints and Politicians: Essays in the Organisation of a Senegalese Peasant Society*. Cambridge, Eng.: Cambridge University Press.

Ottoway, M., and M. Riley. 2006. "Morocco: From Top-Down Reform to Democratic Transition?" Carnegie Papers, no. 71, September.

Philpott, D. 2002. "The Challenge of September 11 to Secularism in International Relations." *World Politics* 55, no. 1, pp. 66–95.

Pinto, P. 2003. "Dangerous Liaisons: Sufism and the States in Syria." In *Crossing Boundaries: From Syria to Slovakia,* ed. S. Jakelic and J. Varsoke. Vienna: IWM Junior Visiting Fellows' Conference, vol. 14.

———. 2007. "Sufism and Political Economy and Morality in Syria." In *Sufism and Politics: The Politics of Spirituality,* ed. Paul Heck. Princeton, N.J.: Markus Weiner.

Porter, G. D. 2008. "Curtailing Illicit and Terrorist Activity in Algeria's Tamanrasset." *Combating Terrorism Center at West Point*. August, Vol. 1.

Ramzi, W., S. Ali, J. Arfaoui, and M. A. Wedoud. 2010. "Sufis Retain Role in Maghreb Islam." *Magharebia*. Available online: http://www.magharebia.com/cocoon/awi/xhtml1/en_GB/features/awi/features/2010/04/08/feature-01.

Riazul, I. 2002. *Sufism in South Asia: Impact on Fourteenth Century Muslim Society*. Karachi: Oxford University Press.

Rozehnal, R. 2004. "Riazul Islam, Sufism in South Asia: Impact on Fourteenth Century Muslim Society." *Journal of Religion* 84, no. 4, pp. 666–67.

Ruedy, J. 2005. *Modern Algeria: The Origins and Development of a Nation*. Bloomington: Indiana University Press.

Safi, O. 2011. "Good Sufi, Bad Muslims." *Sightings,* January 27, 2011. Available online: http://divinity.uchicago.edu/martycenter/publications/sightings/archive_2011/0127.shtml.

Said, A. A., and N. C. Funk. 2001. "Peace in the Sufi Tradition: An Ecology of the Spirit." In *Peace and Conflict Resolution in Islam: Precept and Practice,* ed. A. A. Said, N. C. Funk, and A. S. Kadayifci. Lanham, Md.: University Press of America.

———. 2004. "Sufi Prescriptions for World Politics: A Way to Global Community." "The 'Shakir' World Encounters" Conference, Marrakech, Morocco. 1–19.

Sedwick, M. 2004. "In Search of the Counter-Reformation: Anti-Sufi Stereotypes and the Budshishiyya's Response." In *An Islamic Reformation,* ed. Charles Kurzman and Michaelle Powers. Lanham, Md.: Lexington Books.

Seesemann, R. 2007. "Between Sufism and Islamism: The Tijāniyya and Islamist Rule in the Sudan." In *Sufism and Politics: The Politics of Spirituality,* ed. Paul Heck. Princeton, N.J.: Markus Weiner.

———. 2009. "Three Ibrahims: Literary Production and the Remaking of the Tijāniyya Sufi Order in Twentieth-Century Sudanic Africa." *Die Wels des Islams* 49, nos. 3–4, pp. 299–333.

Seesemann, R., and B. F. Soares. 2009. "'Being as Good Muslims as Frenchmen'; On Marabouts, Colonial Modernity, and the Islamic Sphere in French West Africa." *Journal of Religion in Africa* 39, no. 1, pp. 91–120.

Sidi Chiker. 2011. "King Highlights Symbiosis Between Commandership of the Faithful and Sufi Orders." Second International Sidi Chiker Meeting. Available online: http://www.aktab.ma/sidichikeren/King-highlights-symbiosis-between-Commandership-of-the-Faithful-and-Sufi-Orders_a8.html.

St. John, B. 2008. *Libya: From Colony to Independence.* Oneworld.

Tarzi, S. M. 1991. "Politics of the Afghan Resistance Movement: Cleavages, Disunity, and Fragmentation." *Asian Survey* 31, no. 6, pp. 479–95.

Touahri, Sarah. 2009. "Sufis Hold Global Meeting in Marrakech." *Magharebia*. July 13, 2009. Available online: http://magharebia.com/cocoon/awi/xhtml1/en_GB/features/awi/features/2009/07/13/feature-01?pollresult=yesandanswer=noandid=awi-2010–01–15.

Trimingham, J. S. 1971. *The Sufi Orders in Islam*. New York: Oxford University Press.

U.S. News and World Report. 2005. "The Enemy of My Enemy. . ." Available online: http://www.usnews.com/usnews/news/articles/050425/25roots.b2.htm.

Wehrey, F. 2011. "Libya's Terra Incognita: Who and What Will Follow Qaddafi?" *Foreign Affairs*. Snapshot. February 28, 2011. Available online: http://www.foreignaffairs.com/articles/67551/frederic-wehrey/libyas-terra-incognita?page=2.

Weismann, I. 2005. "The Politics of Popular Religion: Sufis, Salafis, and Muslim Brothers in 20th-Century Hamah." *International Journal of Middle East Studies* 37, pp. 39–58.

Werbner, P. 1996. "The Making of Muslim Dissent: Hybridized Discourses, Lay Preachers, and Radical Rhetoric Among British Pakistanis." *American Ethnologist* 23, no. 1, pp. 102–22.

Witham, L. 1997. "Sheik on a Mission of Peace for Troubled Land." November 1, 1997. *Washington Times*. Retrieved from Major World Publications.

World Tribune 2009. "Algeria Promotes Mystical Variant of Islam to Offset Al Qaida." World Tribune. Available online: http://www.worldtribune.com/worldtribune/WTARC/2009/af_algeria0672_08_23.asp.

Wright, Z. 2005. *On the Path of the Prophet: Ahmad al-Tijāni and the Tariqa Muhammadiya*. Kuala Lumpur, Malaysia: Islamic Book Trust.

Zeghal, M. 2008. *Islamism in Morocco: Religion, Authoritarianism, and Electoral Politics*. Princeton, N.J.: Markus Wiener.

———. 2009. "Politics of Sainthood: Resistance and Mimicry in Postcolonial Morocco." *Critical Inquiry* 35, no. 3, pp. 587–610.

This Filthy Plant: The Inspiration of a Central Sudanic Scholar in the Debate on Tobacco

Dorrit van Dalen, LEIDEN UNIVERSITY INSTITUTE FOR AREA STUDIES

DOI: 10.5192/215409930302227

ABSTRACT

In the seventeenth century, tobacco was fiercely debated from England to Istanbul. Muslim scholars from Bornu and Baghirmi participated in this debate and maintained that smoking was forbidden by divine law, long after their counterparts in the heartlands of Islam allowed it. The question addressed here is why and how the adamant rejection of tobacco in central sudanic Africa was formulated. The study is based on a number of Arabic manuscripts from the region and focuses on a treatise, written around 1700, by Muḥammad al-Wālī b. Sulaymān. It is argued that he was as much inspired by the popular opinion about tobacco in his home-environment as by the writings of scholars from the Middle East. In folktales, tobacco was literally demonised, and the rejection of "pagan" smokers helped to mark new social boundaries. The dominant position regarding smoking was the result of an exchange between islamic learning and popular culture in the region.

The adamant rejection of tobacco "made" the Muslim man in the central Sudanic regions of Bornu and Baghirmi, in the seventeenth and eighteenth centuries.[1] The idea that tobacco, smoked or

[1] Tobacco was also smoked by women in central Sudanic Africa, but little is known about the circumstances. However, since this article is about opinions regarding smoking in general and not about practices, gender aspects are not taken into consideration.

Islamic Africa, VOL. 3, NO. 2, 2012. ISSN 2154-0993. www.islamicafricajournal.org

chewed,[2] did not fit in Islam, was so deeply rooted in the local culture that it inspired at least two scholars[3] from the region to take a position in the debate on tobacco which deviated from that of their peers in the Middle Eastern centers of Islamic learning. In the following pages I will concentrate on the opinion of one of these two scholars and his environment. The texts about tobacco offer a rare opportunity to explore how books, ideas, and narratives from the "global library of Islam," to use a notion of Knut Vikør, were read and adapted, against what background and to what end.

Tobacco crossed the Atlantic Ocean from the Americas to the Old World sometime in the last decade of the sixteenth century. Although initially hailed as a medicine, it aroused deep aversion among many in Europe and in the Levant, an aversion which often took the form of a conviction that smoking or chewing tobacco was against religion. The main objection of opponents in the Muslim countries of the Ottoman Empire was that tobacco "obscured" the mind, like wine does, and was therefore forbidden (*ḥarām*) by divine law. By the end of the seventeenth century, however, after a few decades of heated discussion, most Muslim jurists in the Middle East, North Africa, and the Maghreb had come to the conclusion that obscuring the mind only happened to some smokers, when they imbibed great quantities of tobacco, and that no legal principle applied to proclaim tobacco forbidden.

In what follows, I will first give short descriptions of the debate about tobacco as it was carried on in the Middle East and of the treatise by Muḥammad al-Wālī, a central Sudanic scholar in the seventeenth century. I will then show that he was inspired by the popular opinion about tobacco of the people in his home environment. In this opinion tobacco was more than filthy, it was literally demonized, because society felt deeply threatened by the drug and the habit of smoking. It will be argued that during the period in question, the Muslim communities of Bornu and Baghirmi were "under construction." Their Muslim identity was not yet firmly established, although new converts had an interest in showing a clear Muslim

[2] The central Sudanic texts against tobacco speak of *shurb al-dukhān*, *akl* (chewing) and *istiʿamāl* (using) of *tinbak, ṭibgh, ṭaba'*, and other synonyms.

[3] The second scholar, who is not studied here, is Muḥammad ʿAbd al-Raḥman al-Hajj (d. 1746). He mentioned smoking in a text about shari'ah (*'shurb al-zulāl'*) and those remarks were taken up by a nineteenth-century author in Cairo. John O. Hunwick and R. S. O'Fahey, *Arabic Literature in Africa (ALA)*, vol. II, *The Arabic Writings of Central Sudanic Africa* (Leiden: Brill, 1995), 40, 41.

image of their community as a whole. What they feared was the weakness of their community. The rejection of tobacco and of "pagan" smokers helped to mark new social boundaries. The folktale relating the demonic origins of tobacco emphasized the need to choose between loyalty to the Muslims or to others.

The study is based on a number of manuscripts from present-day northern Nigeria, which are now kept in the Kano collection in the Melville Herskovits Library of Northwestern University in Evanston in the United States, and on manuscripts from the Middle East in the Library of Leiden University in the Netherlands.

The Debate in the Middle East

Because neither the Qur'an nor the traditions (*aḥādith*, singular *ḥadīth*) of the Prophet Muḥammad and his companions mention tobacco, Muslim jurists had to find the answer to the question whether this novelty was allowed or not elsewhere. Generally, they applied the method of analogy (*qiyās*), to extend the validity of a verdict in one of the authoritative sources to tobacco. One of the sources available to them were the principles that the thirteenth-century scholar al-Qarāfī[4] had established about intoxicants, corruptives, and soporifics.

Dozens of jurists gave their opinion in fatwas, and the production of these texts continued for decades. According to Aziz Batran, over seventy fatwas on smoking were produced in the seventeenth century in North Africa alone.[5] One of the best-known texts against tobacco was written in 1616 by a renowned Mālikī professor at the al-Azhar in Cairo, Ibrahīm al-Laqānī (d. 1631).[6] It is a short but fiery treatise which, through the propaganda of al-Laqānī's sons, inspired slightly later opponents like al-Wālī in Bornu and al-Aqḥisārī in Anatolia,[7] and is even quoted in

---

[4] Shihāb al-Dīn Aḥmad b. Idrīs al-Qarāfī al-Ṣanhājī (d. 1285, see Brockelmann, *Geschichte der Arabischen Literatur* [*GAL*] I, 385 and *S* I 665), Mālikī jurist, established the *Qā'ida al-qarāfiyya* about wine and other intoxicants.

[5] Aziz Batran, *Tobacco Smoking Under Islamic Law: Controversy over Its Introduction* (Beltsville: Amana, 2003), 46.

[6] Abū-'l-Imdād Burhān al-Dīn Ibrāhīm b. Ibrāhīm b. Ḥasan b. 'Alī al-Laqānī al-Mālikī. *GAL* II, 316–17. His '*Naṣīhat al-ikhwān bi-jtināb al-dukhān*' was written in 1616.

[7] See Aḥmad al-Aqḥiṣārī, *Against Smoking: An Ottoman Manifesto*, introduction, first edition, and translation by Y. Michot (Leicestershire: Kube, 2010).

a twentieth-century pamphlet from Indonesia.[8] But even contemporaries of al-Laqānī like Mari`ī al-Karmī (d. 1623)[9] argued that although tobacco could be disapproved of in certain circumstances, nothing indicated that it was principally forbidden. Later, famous scholars such as Katib Celebi (1609–1657) in Istanbul and ʿAbd al-Ghanī al-Nābulsī (1641–1731) in Damascus wrote about smoking and found no legal objections.

J. Grehan wrote a study of the reactions to tobacco by rulers and clerics in the Ottoman Empire[10] in which he argues that the aversion and initially very forceful and cruel repression of smoking by a number of Ottoman sultans was caused by the consternation over social and cultural transformations that it accelerated. "In the long term, smoking would help to redefine patterns of social interaction, promoting more relaxed attitudes about pleasure and opening up new avenues for leisure and escapism."[11] Smoking was enjoyed in the also recent invention of coffeehouses. Clerics feared the breakdown of moral restrictions there, and rulers feared that besides coffee and smoke, rebellious ideas were brewed there. Both had an interest in depicting smoking as a habit of the lowest classes, of riffraff.[12]

To emphasize their point about the despicability of tobacco, opponents recounted how it was imported by Christians, and that it was often covered, kneaded, or sprinkled with wine or pig fat, either because Christians liked the taste, or because they intended to harm Muslims. Other stories relate how tobacco was polluted by human or dog's urine, and mixed with or substituted by dung.[13] One of the issues for jurists was whether the impurity of wine disappeared when tobacco was washed, and whether the

[8] I thank Dr. Nico Kapteijn for showing me the pamphlet *'Irshād al-ikhwān li-bayān shurb al-qahwa wa 'l-dukhān,'* by Ihsān Muḥammad Dahlān al-Jampasī al-Kadīrī. It bears no place or date of publication, but the author lived in east Java from 1901 to 1952. Al-Laqānī's popularity among the anti-smoking lobby is somewhat surprising, because ultimately he argued that the legal category applying to smoking was only that of "doubtful" (shubha) matters, not disapproved (makrūh) or forbidden (ḥarām).

[9] Mari`ī b. Yūsuf al-Karmī, d. 1623, was a Hanbalite and wrote '*Tahqīq al-burhān fī shurb al-dukhān*.' *GAL* II 369.

[10] James Grehan, "Smoking and 'Early Modern' Sociability: The Great Tobacco Debate in the Ottoman Middle East (Seventeenth to Eighteenth Centuries)," *American Historical Review* 3 (December 2006): 1352–77.

[11] Ibid., 1353.

[12] See also Rudi Matthee, *The Pursuit of Pleasure: Drugs and Stimulants in Iranian History, 1500–1900* (Princeton, N.J.: Princeton University Press, 2005), 137, 138.

[13] Al-Laqānī, Leiden University Library, Or 8288, f 124b.

smoke of something impure is also impure.[14] But all these only constituted extrinsic reasons for a possible prohibition, whereas the most important question in the legal discussions was whether there were intrinsic reasons to forbid tobacco, for example, because it "obscured" the mind. And that was hard to maintain.

Meanwhile, the popularity of tobacco was unstoppable. Before the second half of the seventeenth century most jurists in the great centers of the Ottoman Empire had come to the conclusion that smoking was allowed (*mubāḥ*). Intellectuals should instead turn their attention to real problems like bribery and corruption, said al-Nābulsī.[15] To the west, the famous Aḥmad Bābā al-Tinbuktī had already set the tune for the scholars of Timbuktu, in favor of tobacco, before 1607. Their colleagues in the Maghreb were divided.[16]

Al-Wali's Deviant Position

The dominant opinion in Bornu and Baghirmi was different. We know this from the author of *Shurb al-Zulāl* (note 3) who condemned smoking in one sentence. But there is another source. Muḥammad al-Wālī, who was one of the leading scholars of his day in central Sudanic Africa during the second half of the seventeenth century, was the author of a whole pamphlet against smoking tobacco.[17] In twenty-three folios his text, entitled *Valid Reasons for the Prohibition of Smoking* (*Al-adilla al-ḥisān fī tahrīm shurb al-dukhān*), presents ten arguments against the habit and the product, followed by a refutation of a treatise by al-Ajhūrī (d. 1656). Al-Ajhūrī, sheikh al-Azhar and one of the highest authorities of the Mālikī school of law in Cairo, had argued before that smoking was not against the law of God.[18] We don't know when the original of *Valid Reasons* was written,

---

[14] See, e.g., al-Ajhūrī in Batran's translation.

[15] Grehan, "Smoking," 1365 and 1369.

[16] Al-Tinbuktī's treatise is entitled '*Al-lamᶜ fī ᵓl- ishāra ilā-hukm tibgh.*' See Batran, *Tobacco Smoking*, 169–90.

[17] Leiden University Library, Or 8362. The Leiden University Library bought it in 1949 from an auction of manuscripts collected by the orientalist P. Herzsohn. The author envisages publishing an edition and translation of the text shortly. Al-Wālī's full name was Muḥammad al-Wālī b. Sulaymān b. Abī Muḥammad al-Wālī al-Fulānī al-Baghirmāwī al-Barnāwī al-Ashᶜarī al-Mālikī.

[18] Nūr al-Dīn ᶜAlī b. Muḥammad b. ᶜAbd al-Rahmān b. ᶜAlī al-Ajhūrī al-Mālikī (1559–1656. *GAL* II 317, *S* II 437), who wrote '*Ghāyat al-bayān liḥill shurb mā lā yughaiyib al-*

nor when al-Wālī was born or died, but one of his fourteen other works is dated in 1688, so the anti-tobacco essay may have been composed in the last decades of the seventeenth century as well. The copy in the University of Leiden, upon which this article is based, was made in 1755, most probably in the Middle East, judging from the handwriting.[19] It is the only copy that is known of this text; no other versions have turned up in African collections.

Muḥammad al-Wālī lived in Baghirmi, southeast of Lake Chad.[20] In the seventeenth century Baghirmi was a marginal kingdom, tributary to the most powerful state of the region in that era, Bornu. But it was far enough away from Bornu to be a safe haven for people who were persecuted by that state's king.[21] The ruling family of Baghirmi, and nominally therefore the whole Barma population,[22] had been Islamized only in the sixteenth century, by missionary Fulani. Al-Wālī himself also belonged to this ethnic group which played such a significant role in the spread of Islam in the whole region. As one of his *nisbas* (names referring to origin) indicates, he also spent some of his time in Bornu, presumably pursuing his studies in the capital Gazargamo, one of the most important centers of learning in West Africa of the time.

A comparison of the authors mentioned by al-Wālī with, on the one hand, the books that according to Hall and Stewart made up the "core-curriculum" of Islamic learning in West Africa,[23] and on the other hand with the West African Arabic Manuscripts Database,[24] shows that al-Wālī read (or listened to the reading of) many more books than most students did, and that

---

ʿaql min al-dukhān,' started this treatise by saying that tobacco was not an intoxicant, and that if it were established that it was also not a soporific or a corruptive, then it would be considered "an absolutely legal substance, the smoke of which is clean and lawful" (translation Batran, *Tobacco Smoking*, 149).

[19] The handwriting is a type of naskh that was written in the Mashriq, in the view of Jan Just Witkam.

[20] Baghirmi is now the name of a prefecture in the same region, in present-day Chad.

[21] Muḥammad Bello in '*Infāq al-Maysur*,' 1812. Edited by Charles. E. J., *Infaku'l Maisuri* (London: Luzac, 1951).

[22] A folk etymology of the name Baghirmi is that this was the land of baggar mia, a hundred cows in Arabic. However, as Kodi Mahamat points out (1992), an important autochthonous (non-Arabic speaking) population group is called Barma. It seems likely that Baghirmi is derived from Barma.

[23] Bruce S. Hall and Charles C. Stewart, "The Historic 'Core Curriculum' and Book Market in West Africa," in *The Transsaharan Book Trade: Manuscript Culture, Arabic Literacy and Intellectual History in Muslim Africa*, ed. G. Krätli and G. Lydon (Brill, 2010), 109–74.

[24] WAAMD, see http://westafricanmanuscripts.org.

he could have found some of these only in Timbuktu or Cairo. It is known that al-Wālī twice made the journey to Mecca, and on his way there spent some time in Cairo. Undoubtedly, he attended lectures in both cities.

Travel is what Muslim scholars did to gain knowledge and prestige, and al-Wālī acquired both. In central Sudanic Africa he enjoyed a great reputation.[25] Some of his works, especially on theology, were copied many times. He wrote an explanation of a theological work which was at the time gaining great influence all over West Africa, al-Sanūsī's *Al-ʿAqīda al-ṣughra* (*The Minor Creed*), also known as *Umm al-barāhīn* (*Mother of Proof*).[26] Al-Wālī's explanation, *Al-Manhaj al-farīd fi maʿrifat 'ilm al-tawḥīd* (*The Peerless Method for Knowledge of Theology*),[27] bears witness to his originality, his affinity with Sufism, and, most of all, his passion for education. A difficult, philosophical work is here "translated" into simple rules and supplemented with basic information about terms and titles in Islam. In fact, the total of al-Wālī's works, including a work on Arabic grammar, advice to young people, and a versification of al-Sanūsī's *Ṣughra* is like a starter kit for Muslims, beginning and advanced—very suitable for the small but growing Muslim population in rural Baghirmi. Some of his theological work has been called cerebral,[28] but texts like *Al-manhaj al-farīd* or *Awṣikum yā maʿshar al-ikhwān* (being advice to use one's time of life well) were clearly adapted to an illiterate public with an enchanted worldview, knowing little Arabic and still learning the basic tenets of Islam. They show the authors' dedication to his "flock." Thus, al-Wālī takes his position in between the cosmopolitan centers of the Islamic world and the African hinterland, or rather perhaps between Muslim learning and the culture of illiterate new converts.

Al-Wālī's treatise against smoking clearly reflects his "double vision." It consists of two parts.[29] The first lists ten reasons why smoking is *ḥarām*.

---

[25] Al-Wālī and his father are the very first scholars mentioned in Muḥammad Bello's *Infāq al-Maysūr*.

[26] *GAL* II 250, *S* II 352.

[27] See *ALA*, Vol. II, 34–37 for a list of al-Wālī's works. Of '*Al-Manhaj al-farīd*' 32 copies still exist in different West African collections.

[28] Mervyn Hiskett about *Urjūza fī ḥudūth al-ʿālam*, in *A History of Islamic Verse* (London: School of Oriental and African Studies, University of London, 1975), 15–16. And Muḥammad Bello writes that al-Wālī's work shows the abundance of his knowledge and intelligence and his skill in science. *Infaku'l Maisuri*, ed. Charles E. J. Whitting (London: Luzac, 1951), 5.

[29] In *Arabic Literature of Africa* the two parts are mentioned as different texts, one of which was supposed to be lost. But the second text should be considered as part of one discourse.

It does so in simple wordings, supported by a host of references to well-known prophetic traditions. One could almost imagine this part being read out by a public crier in a market. The second part then continues with a polemical discussion, paragraph by paragraph, of a treatise on the acceptability of tobacco by the renowned al-Azhar scholar al-Ajhūrī, in a much more scholarly style, in which the syntax is often as complex as the legal argumentation. The general public in Baghirmi would have had no idea what it was about, and the authors referred to would have been unknown to them.

This division in the text seems puzzling, as if it were addressed to two different audiences. But that is not the case. The second part starts with the words "I have just presented ten good reasons," a direct and unambiguous reference to the first part of the work. Because of the style of the second part, and because no copies of the text were found in West African libraries, it seems likely that the treatise as a whole was addressed to an audience of learned jurists in the Middle East, and was produced there. But the first part bears clear traces of an argument that was developed in al-Wālī's home environment.[30]

In spite of the adaptation of the second part to a more intellectual audience, it is remarkable that al-Wālī does not use two arguments that would be most decisive in Islamic law as it was taught in the older centers of learning, namely that smoking would "cloud the mind" and tobacco was impure. But he knew of course that both arguments had been dealt with in the past three quarters of a century, and did not stand their ground. Even his example, al-Laqānī, had admitted that tobacco did not obscure the mind and was therefore not an intoxicant. So al-Wālī writes: "Surely, the things that necessitate its prohibition are other than absence of the mind from smoking it."[31] A bit later he says, in answer to al-Ajhūrī's statement that tobacco is not impure, because the mind is not obscured by it, "there is no connection between a substance obscuring the mind and its being impure."[32] But he is careful enough to refrain from saying that tobacco ís impure. Instead, his ten objections were that smoking was *bidʿa* (an unlaw-

---

[30] It resembles, e.g., manuscript Falke 1850, Melville Herskovits Library, Northwestern University (NU). This manuscript comes from the same region, and probably from the same time. It also mentions al-Ajhūrī and al-Laqānī, and many other earlier authors, but no later ones. It lists many of the same arguments against smoking, and opens with al-Wālī's poem *Awṣikum ya maʿshar al-ikhwān*. It will be interesting to find out if this text could in fact be by the hand of al-Wālī himself.

[31] Or 8362, f 9b.

[32] Or 8362, f 12b.

ful innovation), it distracts the attention from religion, it stinks and harms the body, it is copying a habit of heathens (who introduced tobacco), it is filthy, it makes one drowsy (although it cannot be characterized as an intoxicant, it is still a soporific), it involves a waste of money, smoke is one of God's punishment on the Day of Judgment (and who would want to associate with that), and smoking is "unmanly."

All these arguments had been mentioned by others, although few listed so many in one text. But compared to others al-Wālī puts a lot of emphasis on his opinion that tobacco is filthy or disgusting, *khabīth*. The words *khabīth* and its synonyms *shanī'* and *qabīḥ* occur fifteen times within the first sixteen folios. Now *khabīth* is a word that plays a role in the Qur'an. In sura 7:157, for example, God forbids people to consume what is *khabīth*. A few others had called tobacco *khabīth* too: al-Laqānī and another very early writer on the topic, a Ḥanafī scholar in Medina named al-Nāfī[33] and perhaps some others, since al-Karmī reacted to it. But in neither of the four law schools is *khabīth* a legal category. It does not imply any sanction, as al-Karmī had already pointed out before the first quarter of the seventeenth century was over. He and others did consider tobacco *karīh*, disliked or repugnant, and deducted from that the legal verdict of smoking as *makrūh*, disapproved. But that would not have helped al-Wālī, who aimed for more, and wanted its total condemnation as *ḥarām*. Consequently, he does not even use the word *karīh*.

Al-Wālī also stresses the incompatibility of smoking with "manliness" or decency, that is, *murū'a*. *Murū'a* is a complex term that is associated with the honor of an individual or a tribe, with the observance of duties connected to family ties, and—notably in West Africa—with self-restraint and the control of emotions.[34] Thus, when the term *murū'a* occurs in later[35] manuscripts about smoking (Falke 1040, f 15; Falke 1101, f 19), it is in contrast with such antisocial behavior observed among smokers as fooling around and dancing, lowering oneself, being inferior for having sub-

---

[33] See Felix Klein-Franke, "No Smoking Paradise: The Habit of Tobacco Smoking Judged by Muslim Law," *Le Muséon* 106 (1993): 155–92.

[34] See the chapter on *murū'a* and *dīn* in Ignaz Goldziher, *Muslim Studies* (London: George Allen and Unwin, 1967), 22. See for an example of *murū'a* in West Africa at the beginning of the nineteenth century: ʿAbdallāh b. Muḥammad dan Fodio who writes that after a certain military victory only shariʿa and "the chain of *murū'a* kept men from fighting over the booty." *Tazyīn al-waraqāt*, ed. and trans. M. Hiskett (Ibadan University Press, 1963), 116.

[35] These manuscripts mention names referring to members of the Tijāniyya movement, and therefore must be of the nineteenth century or later.

stituted one's brains with smoke, eating in public (all mentioned in Falke 1101 and 1040), and indulging in calumny and wild hilarious conduct (al-Fakkoun)[36]—in short, the behavior of riffraff (*al-raʿāʿ*).

In another work[37] al-Wālī himself even mentioned smoking tobacco as one of the capital sins, together with adultery, stealing, slander, and defamation. That was a far cry, which he did not repeat in the legal discourse of *Valid Reasons*. But in Islamic law, none of al-Wālī's other ten arguments and concerns suffice to proclaim something forbidden. He knew it, and all the hadiths (about fire, for example) he drags in do not really make up for the weakness of his plea. The question is, why he was so eager to make an impossible point?

Obviously, al-Wālī had a personal aversion to smoking. But so did others, who saw no legal indication for a prohibition.[38] On the other hand, the motives of other opponents to smoking seem different from al-Wālī's. Someone like al-Aqḥiṣārī, for example, was inspired by puritanical ideas about the reform of Islam as propagated by Ibn Taymiyya. Such puritanism, however, was not what inspired al-Wālī, who tended much more toward Sufism.[39] What inspired him to compose a text in which the word *khabīth* is central did not come from scholars in the older centers of Islamic learning, but from common people in his own homeland.

A Folktale about the Devil's Urine

Near the end of his essay, al-Wālī mentions a strange story about tobacco, which was presented as a hadith. This story was first noted—as we know from the Algerian Mālikī jurist al-Fakkūn (d. 1663)—in Algeria, around 1600.[40] Al-Fakkūn described it in 1616, and mentions four elements:

---

[36] In Batran, *Tobacco Smoking,* see below, p. 6.

[37] *Al-manhaj al-farīd.*' Hunwick collection manuscript 178, p. 11.

[38] For example, al-Karmī and, initially, al-Nābulsī (who turned into a smoker later). The latter wrote *Al-Ṣulḥ bayna al-ikhwān fī ḥukm ibāhāt al-dukhān* in 1682. *GAL* II 345, *S* II 473.

[39] See also both Hiskett and Levtzion, who write that the jihad of Uthman dan Fodio was not inspired by Wahhabism, as some authors have suggested, but rather by local history. Mervyn Hiskett, "An Islamic Tradition of Reform in the western Sudan," *Bulletin of the School of Oriental and African Studies* (*BSOAS*) vol. 25 (1962); Nehemia Levtzion, "Islam in African and Global Contexts: Adventures in Comparative Studies of Islam," in *Islam in Africa and the Middle East: Studies on Conversion and Renewal,* by N. Levtzion (Aldershot: Ashgate Variorum, 2006).

[40] By a certain al-Susi, probably Abu ʿAbd Allah al-Susi, who died in 1614. It seems plausible that al-Fakkūn means him, although he also describes him as someone "who did not rise to the level of an author . . . because his reasoning was defective." Batran, *Tobacco Smoking,* 216.

Tobacco was created from the urine of Iblīs.[41]

The Prophet has said that smokers do not belong to his *ummah.*

The Prophet predicted smoking to Abū Hurayra.

It was when God told Iblīs that he would have no authority over His people (Q. 15:42) that he urinated, from shock.

The first two elements form the core of the narrative, and in other versions these are combined: there it is the prophet himself who says that tobacco grows from the devil's urine. The last statement, a *vaticidium ex eventu,* "is simply arbitrary and nonsensical," says al-Fakkūn.[42]

As far as I know, this story has not survived in the Maghreb or the Middle East. But there are a number of versions of it in the Kano collection of Arabic manuscripts from the region of present-day northern Nigeria and west Chad, where it still survives today. With their repetition, irregular handwriting, and spelling mistakes, they are clearly the deposit of stories that were passed on orally, among people who were not very skilled in Arabic, presumably rural. The shortest compilation runs as follows:

> Bismillah and greetings to our lord Muḥammad, his family, companions, wives and slave-girls. This "book" is communicated by the noble [Prophet], [when] consulted by 'Alī b. Abī Ṭālib. On account of the prophet, God bless him and grant him salvation: all inanimate nature is pure, except this one plant that grows in the urine of Iblīs and is from the bottom of the hell. It is more reprehensible than wine. He who eats of this plant, the prophet says that he rejects him from him and that he is not of his umma. For he who chews it is an unbeliever. There is no peace for him, nor religion, nor jihad and he is damned in the Torah as well as in the Gospel, in the Book of Psalms and in the Furqān.[43]
>
> God, the benevolent, the exalted, said that vicious things are forbidden to them: wine, gambling, calumny and pigs and adultery and slander. These are the first things that are evil to him. On account of Abū Hurayra[44]

---

[41] Iblīs is an alternative name for the Devil, especially associated with the story of the creation of the world. See the *Encyclopaedia of Islam, second edition,* "Iblīs."

[42] Batran, *Tobacco Smoking,* 253.

[43] Synonym of Qur'an, see below.

[44] A companion of the Prophet. In canonical hadith collections, he is one of the transmitters of the Prophet's words "he who eats of this plant (garlic) should not approach our mosque and should not harm us with the odor of it," which was used as an argument against smoking.

> may God be pleased with him, from the prophet who said: "Beware of this plant." He said it is [like] wine, more than wine.
>
> It is told on account of Abū Ḥudhayfa, may God be pleased with him, that Abū Ḥudhayfa said that he went out with a party of the Messenger of God and [said] "I saw this plant and [the prophet] said: "This is from Iblīs' urine." He also said: "A time will come after me, when they will drink this plant and be drunk from it and will err from the path of God. For them will be punishment according to the verse from the Book of God. And he who says to them 'leave this plant!' he will be an enemy to them.[45] But they are the worst people and I am far from them.'"
>
> ʿAlī b. Abī Ṭālib said: "The messenger from God, peace be upon him, said: 'he who eats from this plant belongs to the depths of hell. May God, the Exalted, curse him – He does not care.'"[46]
>
> ʿAlī said: "There is no peace for them, do not befriend them, do not sit down with them, do not greet them, do not help them, do not laugh with them."[47]

The rest of this manuscript is lost, but other versions continue with a list of forms of social interaction that should not take place with smokers. The element of the original version, where the prophet said that smokers do not belong to his *ummah,* is here converted into an order to his *ummah* to actively exclude users of tobacco.

Al-Wālī says he believes that al-Ajhūrī refers to this story when he writes that "the oft-repeated traditions [to refute tobacco] are fabrications . . . concocted in contemporary times"[48] and admits that al-Ajhūrī would be right. But at the same time he repeats the information with the unquestioned context of the Quranic verse.

> Among [the *aḥādith* that are fabricated] we must mention the derogation of tobacco as coming from the urine of Iblīs, may God curse him. When he was terrified after hearing the words of the Highest, "as for My servants, you have no power over them,"[49] he was shocked and he uri-

---

[45] Compare the words of the Algerian al-Fakkūn who wrote in 1616 that when he admonished people not to smoke, he was mocked and scandalized. See Batran, *Tobacco Smoking,* 209.

[46] Compare the *ḥadith qudsī*, "These to hell and I do not care, and those to paradise, and I do not care."

[47] Manuscript Falke 2017, Melville Herskovits Library, NU.

[48] Batran, *Tobacco Smoking,* 157.

[49] Sura 15:42.

> nated and this plant sprang up from his urine. And the *ḥadith* related by Ḥudhayfa ibn al-Yamān [must be mentioned], and he said: "I went out with the prophet, God bless him, and he saw a plant and shook his head. I asked, O messenger of God, why do you shake your head? He told me: "A time will come to the people when they will drink[50] from the leaves of this plant." And there are other *aḥādith* that they relate like these, of which we don't know the source."[51]

This is not a sharp denunciation, but rather shows that al-Wālī is taking the feelings seriously of those around him who did believe the story of tobacco's origin in the devil's urine. In another, contemporary anti-tobacco manuscript from the region, Falke 1850,[52] this demonic origin was presented as a fact. In *Valid Reasons* al-Wālī shows that, although he knows that tobacco was not introduced into the Islamic world before the tenth century after the hegira, he is still deeply imbued with the idea that the herb is intrinsically disgusting. The question now is what the essence of this idea was.

Other versions of the hadith even equate tobacco with idolatry, the worst of sins. And in later anti-tobacco texts there are comparisons of smokers with dung beetles, allusions to the stench of an anus, riffraff, uncivilized behavior, and not heeding the law. Altogether, it seems that in the course of time, no means were spared to literally demonize tobacco and depict it as not merely besmeared with urine, but intrinsically soiled by it. Significantly, the sanction on smoking was not punishment in the hereafter, but being ostracized here and now. All this effort suggests that these central Sudanese societies felt deeply threatened by smoking tobacco.[53] The next step then, is to find out what this threat was.

The Threat of Tobacco

Grehan as well as Matthee pointed out that in the Middle East, tobacco caused fears of social disruption when it was first introduced. In the

---

[50] In Arabic the term for smoking is "to drink smoke," *shurb al-dukhān*.

[51] 8362, folio 19a.

[52] See note 30.

[53] In neighboring Sokoto the attitude of the Qadiriyya leaders toward tobacco was completely different. ʿAbdallah dan Fodio wrote a chapter (called "Teasing," *tankīt*) on tobacco in which he listed its benefits. I thank Prof. Murray Last for drawing my attention to this chapter in *Ḍiyāʾ al-siyāsāt wa-fatāwī ʾl-nawāzil mimmā huwa fī furūʾal-dīn min al-masāʾil*.

nineteenth-century travelogues of European travelers in central Sudanic Africa there is nothing to be found of coffeehouses or smoking-holes like they existed in Ottoman centers or the Maghreb, where vagabonds were wasting away and an urban underclass could concoct schemes against its masters. But some of the same worries seem to have troubled people here too. In the manuscript Falke 1850, for example, it says: "[smoking tobacco] keeps the mind from caring about matters. If a person is learned, it keeps him away from learning and work and from seeking refuge [with God]. If he is a worshiper, it keeps him from worship. If he is a slave, it keeps him from serving his master. If he is a merchant, it diminishes what is his and keeps him from his occupations. For the smoker drowns his heart with love for it and drowns his time night and day with smoking and with craving for it. . . . Is there worse *fitna* than this?"[54] Smoking perturbs the social order, it leads to *jahiliyya* (lit: ignorance, ff 2a and 4b), to chaos.

Admittedly, this concern is not explicitly expressed in other texts from the region. Very frequent, however, are the associations of smoking with riffraff (*al-raʿāʿ*), as they were also made in texts from the Maghreb, North Africa, and the Middle East. In all these regions, riffraff or people of the lowest standing were African slaves. A certain al-Isḥāqī, for example, said that smoking was the habit of contemptible Sudanese and people of low standing.[55] Sudan, literally meaning "black," had been a vague geographical designation referring to sub-Sahara Africa ever since the first Arabic writings on the area. But it also had a negative connotation. Hunwick explained that there existed in the Arab-Muslim culture (in Africa) a very old "simplistic equation of *black* equals *slave* equals *inferior.*"[56] African Muslims themselves often used the words for "black" and "unbeliever" as synonyms. The famous Muḥammad Bello, one of the leaders of the Sokoto jihad of the beginning of the nineteenth century, wrote about the lands south of Sokoto that "the inhabitants there are Sudanese, Islam has not spread there" and that in Mali lived "Christians, Jews and Sudanese."[57] Black did (and does) not in the first place refer to the color of skin. On the

[54] Falke 1850, f 6b.

[55] Muḥammad b. ʿAbdal Muʾtī al-Isḥāqī. Batran, *Tobacco Smoking*, 58.

[56] John O. Hunwick, *West Africa and the Arab World* (J. B. Danquah Memorial Lectures, series 21, Ghana Academy of Arts and Sciences, 1991).

[57] In the translation by E. J. Arnett, *The Rise of the Sokoto Fulani. Being a Paraphrase and in Some Parts Translation of the Infaku'l Maisuri of Sultan Mohammed Bello* (Kano, 1922?), 12 and 137.

other hand, people with a black skin were easily tainted by the designation "sudani" in the sense of pagan. That was dangerous, because it made them eligible for slavery.

Slavery was extensive in this part of Africa. Before merchants from North Africa and later Europe bought them, slaves seem to have been used by rulers in the region to colonize land that was hard to cultivate without them. Then, starting in the seventh century, they became the most important "commodity" in the trade of the eastern parts of central Sudanic Africa with Libya and Morocco. In the eighteenth and nineteenth centuries European travelers learned that they constituted the main and indispensable labor force for agriculture in the region, as well as valuta in some cases. Leo Africanus (sixteenth century) noticed that the king of Bornu had no other income than the slaves he procured from neighboring countries.[58] And Bornu in turn was raided by others.[59] Numerous sources reveal how tribes throughout the region carried out yearly raids on their neighbors, to supplement poor harvests or even just to celebrate someone's homecoming. Slave raids were a constant danger for populations living on the margins of Bornu, Wadai, and other Islamic states. According to Islamic law, Muslims could not be made into slaves, and sometimes that could be a reason for conversion.[60]

In central Sudanic Africa conversion was not an individual matter. "Muslim" was a collective label: a population was Muslim when its rulers were Muslim, and an individual was considered Muslim if his whole community had a firm Muslim identity.[61] The seventeenth century saw the start of a movement of Islam from towns to rural areas. For centuries Islam had

[58] Nehemia Levtzion, "Slavery and the Slave Trade in the Early States of Bilād as-Sūdān," in *Islam in Africa and the Middle East: Studies on Conversion and Renewal*, by Levtzion (Aldershot: Ashgate Variorum, 2006).

[59] Victor N. Low, *Three Nigerian Emirates* (Evanston, Ill.: Northwestern University Press, 1972), 124.

[60] Conversion to Islam as a strategy to escape slavery is explicit, for example, in Dixon Denham, *Travels and Discoveries in Northern and Central Africa in 1822, 1823 and 1824/ Denham, Clapperton and Oudney*, vol. 2 (London, 1831), 40, 41.

[61] A very precise discussion about the legality and illegality of slavery is a famous text by Aḥmad Bābā al-Tinbuktī, *Miʿrāj al-ṣu'ūd ilā nayl ḥukm majlūb al-sūd*. For a translation, see B. Barbour and M. Jacobs, "The Miʾraj: A Legal Treatise on Slavery by Ahmad Baba," in John R. Willis, *Slaves and Slavery in Muslim Africa*, vol. 1 (London: Frank Cass, 1985). Because it was legal to obtain slaves from "lands of unbelief" (in principle when they were captured during a "jihād" and refused Islam, but this principle was flexible) Aḥmad Bābā and others gave lists of countries of unbelievers, from where it was legal to obtain slaves.

been a matter of the elites only, of rulers who attached ulama to their courts in order to strengthen their authority. Then Islam started to spread outside the towns and from families of rulers and merchants to farmers, in all of west Africa.[62] Although conversion started with the mere utterance of the Muslim creed and in some cases outward signs like a head cover, a Muslim identity did not come to communities as easily as it might seem. One reason was that all those whose economy was based on slaves had an interest in defining neighboring communities as unbelievers.[63]

Also, converted people often did "lapse back" to their traditional religion, or they did not really give up all the rituals of veneration of the spirits and gods who had always decided about the fertility of their land and rivers and animals, and about the health or punishment of people. One of the processes that marks the social history of central Sudanic Africa, especially in the sixteenth to nineteenth centuries, is the competition between Islam and traditional religions or animism, and between different types of political authority based on either one.[64] Not every inhabitant of villages that converted followed the leader who turned to Islam. Even at the end of the nineteenth century important parts of the population of "Muslim" villages in Bornu were non-Muslim.[65] The non-Muslims lived in their own quarter of a village, but otherwise there were no significant differences in lifestyle between Muslims and non-Muslims. All this meant that the unity and force of Muslim society was unstable, even in the Sokoto caliphate[66] and a fortiori in Bornu, Baghirmi, and other regions in present-day Chad.[67]

[62] Nehemia Levtzion 2006, VII.

[63] See Denham, *Travels and Discoveries,* 2:40, 41.

[64] Finn Fuglestad, "A Reconsideration of Hausa History Before the *Jihād,*" *Journal of African History* 19, no. 3 (1978): 319–39. See also the article about the integration of Islamic elements into African societies by Nehemia Levtzion, "Sociopolitical Roles of Muslim Clerics and Scholars in West Africa," in *Comparative Social Dynamics,* ed. Erik Cohen et al. (Boulder: Worldview, 1985).

[65] Victor N. Low, *Three Nigerian Emirates,* 1972.

[66] A sense of the proximity of paganism as the alternative option pervades Muḥammad Bello's *Infāq al-maysūr*. "I live on the margin of emptiness, in the Sudan, where paganism and dark ignorance prevail," he writes. One of the main issues of the writers of the Sokoto caliphate was differentiating between true and false Muslims. See Murray Last, *The Sokoto Caliphate* (Longmans, London, 1967); and Humphrey Fisher, "The Fulani 'Jihād,'" review of *Tazyīn al-Waraqāt*, by Abdallah ibn Muhammad, ed. and trans. Mervyn Hiskett, *Journal of African History* 7, no. 2 (1966): 344–47.

[67] For examples in Bornu in the nineteenth century, see Gustav Nachtigal, *Sahara and Sudan* (C. Hurst & Company, London, 1980) vols. 2 and 3. For Baghirmi, see Kodi Maha-

Choosing an Identity

And yet these populations needed the image of Muslim communities, if they wanted to be left alone by slave-raiding neighbors. They had to make a choice between a culture of Islam and their old customs and be clear about it, in a society where being Muslim had such serious implications. It is not suggested that not smoking was enough to present a community as Muslim. But in this context, the struggle against tobacco may be seen as a struggle against the temptation for Muslims to fall back to non-Islamic loyalties.

The "hadith" about tobacco helped to create an identity for the *umma.* It did so not only in religious terms, but also in terms of actual customs. Other options to do the same were limited. Muslims were allowed and sometimes ordered to wear a turban, but otherwise the clothing of (rural) Muslims and non-Muslims was the same. Women had the same tasks, and remaining in their house or courtyard was something rural women could not afford. Changing burial rites was psychologically and socially difficult,[68] and even praying five times a day, one of the pillars of Islam and a religious obligation, was and is not easy in a farming life, to name a few other options. Smoking, however, was something one could choose not to do. Indulging in it—which must have happened, or we would not have so many texts on the topic—could be seen as a penchant for a novelty which came literally and figuratively speaking from the other direction, from the Christians and Jews in the West. Using tobacco therefore could serve as a sign of failing in loyalty to a community under construction.

The threat of tobacco was the threat of the attraction of an alternative identity. The rejection of smoking offered an opportunity to mark the boundary between Muslims and others. The sanction of ostracizing smokers gave an opportunity to strengthen the unity of the Muslim community.

---

mat, *Dignitaires et titulaires: Quelques aspects des institutions Baghirmiennes au xixme siecle* (Paris: Conférences et Documents Aresae, 1992). For the Zaghawa of northern Chad, see Marie-Josée Tubiana, *Survivances pré-islamiques en pays Zaghawa* (Paris: Institut d'Ethnologie, Musée de l'Homme, 1964).

[68] Murray Last explains why it was easier for people in densely populated areas than for farmers to convert to Islam. Murray Last, "Economical Aspects of Conversion in Hausaland, Nigeria," in *Conversion to Islam,* by N. Levtzion (New York: Holmes and Meyer, 1979). From a text about *bidʿa* by Uthmān dan Fodio (Manuscript Hunwick 151, Melville Herskovits Library, NU) it appears that even in Sokoto people were not very willing to give up their traditional ways of burying.

And the description of tobacco as filthy and stinking was an opportunity to defend the choice for Islam.

Making that choice is what the story about the devil's piss is all about. The theme of choosing, or more precisely of the distinction between good and bad, is amply represented in all the versions that we have. The person who relates to Abū Hurayra or Abū Ḥudhayfa that the prophet said that tobacco grows in the devil's urine and that smokers should be excluded from the community is ʿAlī b. Abī Ṭālib. He was not only a close relative to the Prophet Muḥammad, he is also known and usually depicted as the man with the double-edged sword, which separates Muslims from unbelievers, as Dhū al-Faqār, the Purifier. In one manuscript with "tobacco *aḥadith*" ʿAlī b. Abī Ṭālib is given the name al-Karār, the Assaulter, "because he slew heathens with a sword in jihad."[69] Second, in all versions of the narrative, the word Furqān is used instead of Qurʾan. Furqān is a synonym for Qurʾan, but is used to evoke the meaning of the Book that distinguishes good from evil.

Conclusion

In Bornu and Baghirmi of the seventeenth and eighteenth centuries, the spread of Islam played a role in creating new partitions between populations. At the same time it provided the narratives that helped to define new loyalties. Confronted with the arrival of the new foreign commodity of tobacco on the one hand, that coincided with a period of redefinition of allegiances, rural people in central Sudanic Africa used these narratives to fabricate a hadith about tobacco, to help them construct their identity as Muslims. In doing so they chose a point of view regarding tobacco that was different from that of mainstream Muslim jurists of that time.

By the end of the seventeenth century, the meaning that tobacco had acquired there was so deeply rooted in the local culture that it convinced a scholar like Muḥammad al-Wālī of the necessity to point out to his colleagues in the Middle Eastern centers of Islamic learning that they were straying from God's path. His remarkable and rather headstrong position in the "international" debate on tobacco was determined by the lens through which he read their legal works: the lens of his local culture.

Al-Wālī's own text shows that he was well aware of the arguments and conventions of the debate in circles of the most respected jurists. Muslims

---

[69] Paden 76, ff 4 and 6. Herskovits Library.

from the geographical margins of the Islamic world who traveled to the Middle East have often been understood to find there "what seemed to them true Islam, but which often contrasted with the Islam in their homeland, which now appeared to them utterly polluted by influences of popular customs and pre-Islamic practices."[70] But the example that was briefly presented here shows that Muslims living on the periphery did not always consider the Islam of the center to be more true.

Works Cited

Primary Sources

Anonymous manuscripts Paden 76, 204, 2017.

Anonymous manuscripts Falke 1040, 1101, 1850.

ʿAbd al-Qādir b. al-ʿAydarūs, *Safwat al-safwa fī bayān ḥukm al-qahwa*. Or 8267, Leiden.

Dedeh, M.*Risāla fi ḥaqq al-qahwa*, Or 682, Leiden.

Uthman dan Fodio, Hunwick 151.

(al-Karmī) Mar'ī b. Yūsuf al-Karmī al-Ḥanbalī, *Taḥqīq al-burhān fī shurb al-dukhān*. Or 6275 (ff 49-55).

(al-Laqānī) Ibrāhīm al-Laqānī, *Naṣīḥat al-ikhwān bi-jtināb al-dukhān*. Or 8288h (ff 117-138).

(Al-Wālī) Muḥammad al-Wālī b. Sulaymān b. Abī Muḥammad al-Wālī al-Fulānī al-Bāghirmāwī al-Barnāwī al-Ashʿarī al-Mālikī, *Al-Adilla al-ḥisān fī bayān taḥrīm shurb al-dukhān*. Or 8362, Leiden.

———. *Al-Manhaj al-farīd fī maʾrifat ʾilm al-tawḥīd*. Hunwick 178 and Ibadan 82/48.

Secondary Sources

Al-Aqḥiṣārī, Aḥmad. *Against Smoking: An Ottoman Manifesto*. Introduction, first edition, and translation by Y. Michot. Leicestershire: Kube, 2010.

Barbour, B., and M. Jacobs. "The Miʿraj: A Legal Treatise on Slavery by Ahmad Baba." In *Slaves and Slavery in Muslim Africa*, vol. 1, J. R. Willis (ed.). London: Frank Cass, 1985.

Batran, Aziz. *Tobacco Smoking Under Islamic Law: Controversy over Its Introduction*. Beltsville: Amana, 2003.

Bello, M. *Infāq al-Maysūr* . Ed. Charles E. J. Whitting. London: Luzac, 1951.

[70] Annemarie Schimmel, *Mystical Dimensions of Islam* (Chapel Hill: University of North Carolina Press, 1975).

Dan Fodio, ʻAbdallāh b. Muḥammad. *Tazyīn al-waraqāt.* Edited and translated by M. Hiskett. Ibadan University Press, 1963.

Denham, Dixon. *Travels and Discoveries in Northern and Central Africa in 1822, 1823 and 1824/Denham, Clapperton and Oudney*, vol 2. London, 1831.

Fisher, Humphrey. "The Fulani 'Jihād.'" Review of *Tazyīn al-Waraqāt,* by Abdallah ibn Muhammad, edited and translated by M. Hiskett. *Journal of African History* 7, no. 2 (1966).

Fuglestad, Finn. "A Reconsideration of Hausa History Before the *Jihād*." *Journal of African History* 19, no. 3 (1978).

Goldziher, Ignaz. *Muslim Studies*. London: George Allen and Unwin, 1967.

Grehan, James. "Smoking and 'Early Modern' Sociability: The Great Tobacco Debate in the Ottoman Middle East (Seventeenth to Eighteenth Centuries)." *American Historical Review*, vol. 3 (December 2006).

Hall, Bruce S., and Charles Stewart. "The Historic 'Core Curriculum' and Book Market in West Africa." In *The Transsaharan Book Trade:. Manuscript Culture, Arabic Literacy and Intellectual History in Muslim Africa,* G. Krätli and G. Lydon (eds). Leiden: Brill, 2010.

Hiskett, Mervyn. *A History of Islamic Verse*. London: School of Oriental and African Studies, University of London, 1975.

———. "An Islamic Tradition of Reform in the Western Sudan." In *Bulletin of the School of Oriental and African Studies*, vol. 25 (1962).

Hunwick, John O. *West Africa and the Arab World.* J. B. Danquah Memorial Lectures, series 21, Ghana Academy of Arts and Sciences, 1991.

Hunwick, John O., and R. S. O'Fahey. *Arabic Literature in Africa,* vol. 2, *The Arabic Writings of Central Sudanic Africa*. Leiden: Brill, 1995.

Klein-Franke, Felix. "No Smoking Paradise: The Habit of Tobacco Smoking Judged by Muslim Law." *Le Muséon*, vol. 106 (1993): 155–92.

Last, Murray. "Economical Aspects of Conversion in Hausaland, Nigeria." In *Conversion to Islam,* Nehemia. Levtzion (ed.). New York: Holmes and Meyer, 1979.

Levtzion, Nehemia. "Islam in African and Global Contexts: Adventures in Comparative Studies of Islam." In *Islam in Africa and the Middle East: Studies on Conversion and Renewal,* by N. Levtzion. Aldershot: Ashgate Variorum, 2006.

———. "Slavery and the Slave Trade in the Early States of Bilād as-Sudan." In *Islam in Africa and the Middle East. Studies on Conversion and Renewal,* by N. Levtzion. Aldershot: Ashgate Variorum, 2006.

———. "Sociopolitical Roles of Muslim Clerics and Scholars in West Africa."

In *Comparative Social Dynamics,* ed. E. Cohen et al. Boulder: Worldview 1985.

Low, Victor N. *Three Nigerian Emirates*. Evanston, Ill.: Northwestern University Press, 1972.

Mahamat, Kodi. *Dignitaires et titulaires: Quelques aspects des institutions Baghirmiennes au xixme siecle*. Paris: Conférences et Documents Aresae, 1992.

Matthee, Rudi. *The Pursuit of Pleasure: Drugs and Stimulants in Iranian History, 1500–1900*. Princeton, N.J.: Princeton University Press, 2005.

Schimmel, Annemarie. *Mystical Dimensions of Islam*. Chapel Hill: University of North Carolina Press, 1975.

Tubiana, Marie-Josée. *Survivances pré-islamiques en pays Zaghawa*. Paris: Institut d'Ethnologie, Musée de l'Homme, 1964.

BOOK REVIEWS

DOI: 10.5192/215409930302249

J. Millard Burr and Robert O. Collins. *Sudan in Turmoil: Hasan al-Turabi and the Islamist State, 1989–2003.* Princeton, N.J.: Markus Wiener Publishers, 2010, $28.95. 340 pp. including bibliography, 1 map, and index.

"Bad Company" in Khartoum

The title of this book could apply to the last fifty-six years of Sudan's history. The book is a reissue in the United States of a book published in the Netherlands in 2003 under the title *Revolutionary Sudan: Hasan al-Turabi and the Islamist State, 1989–2000.* This new edition includes a new final chapter entitled "The Murshid Forsaken," and an afterword by one of Robert Collins's doctoral students, Ohio State University historian Ahmad A. Sikainga. A prominent American historian of Sudan, Robert Collins died in 2008.

In that the book itself has an intriguing history, it is interesting to read it in the context of all that has transpired in Sudan since its first publication. The authors provide a meticulously detailed account of Hasan al-Turabi's decades-old project to turn Sudan into an Islamist state; those details help to explain subsequent events in Sudan and in the wider Middle East as well, and provide strong evidence for claims of Turabi's Svengali-like influence over the region. With a bibliography that is only two pages long, the book is primarily based on news reports from a wide variety of sources and personal communications to the well-connected authors. This is not an academic study in the sense of theoretically based arguments tested against evidence in the field, or even a biography of Turabi. It is an excellent timeline of Turabi's influence over the 1989 coup in Khartoum that brought Omer Hassan el-Bashir to power, and the many ways in which Turabi consolidated his power, and lost it, by entangling Sudan in regional and Muslim world alliances. As the authors state, it is the story of how Turabi's charisma helped to "transform a secular state into an Islamic theocracy by a military coup d'etat" (p. 87).

In that most of the material in the book is from published news sources, and in that the book was originally published in 2003, it is not new

Islamic Africa, VOL. 3, NO. 2, 2012. ISSN 2154-0993. www.islamicafricajournal.org

information that is the appeal of the work. Rather, it is a useful review in concise prose—that shows no favor for the regime in Khartoum—of the remarkable network of allies and alliances that Turabi established while in and out of prison. The use of exclamation points, like on p. 164 in describing budding Sudan-Iran ties, reveals a bit of the bias and the *Africa Confidential* style of the book.

The authors, though, know the region very well and leave us with intriguing questions like, if Turabi's in-law Osama bin Laden was buying guest houses in Peshawar in the 1990s, why were we surprised to find him in one nearby in Abbottabad in 2011? At the same time, in that it is more of a chronology than an analysis, we do not get a detailed sense of the character of the main actors here, like Turabi.

This is a useful reference book, in effect, concluded with a brief and excellent chapter by Professor Ahmad Sikainga, written after the death of his mentor, Robert Collins, which describes events through the end of 2009. It fills out the picture of Sudan's very messy politics by demonstrating how this nation, referred to by Trimingham in the 1940s as the "Islamic fringe," became a key player in the Muslim world under Turabi's crafty guidance.

Steve Howard, Ohio University

Bruce S. Hall. *A History of Race in Muslim West Africa (1600–1960)*. Cambridge, Eng.: Cambridge University Press, 2011, $90 hardcover. 358 pp. including maps and illustrations.

The idea that Africans are solely the victims of European and American racism is still a firmly engrained doxa. Scholars who analyze the racial discourse underlying African social relations outside the colonial construct run the risk of being wrongly accused of racism themselves if they do not tread very carefully. Therefore, the historiography of the Sahel has remained in dire need of a critical analysis of the local construction of race for a long time. In recent years a number of such studies have indeed been written, for Sudan notably, but none have the historical depth this work has.

Hall's central argument is that racial discourses and social constructs as we now find them in the Sahel predate colonial penetration by centuries and that, if we want to understand these, we need to study the intellectual history of the region in depth to unfold the layers of racial discourse as they developed. Only then will we be able to understand the influence of the last layer of racial discourse, constructed under colonial rule, and the impact it has on post-colonial political language. To do so, Hall departs from the nominalist stance on racial discourse. While there might not be a single term to denote "race" in many societies, the layered historical processes of social and political inclusion and exclusion we now call "race" can well be discerned and should be studied historically wherever we find them. Hall does so for the West African Sahel over the past four centuries, and therewith gives us a solid study that will enable future scholars to compare racial constructs on a global scale in the *longue durée*.

Although there are notable differences between racial constructs in the Sahel and the Atlantic world, there are important similarities between them too. The most important is that racial discourse is linked to structural juridical inequality and political domination, especially in the practical shape of the enslavement of black people. This is then defended by a moral justification based on an idea of "natural inferiority." How this "natural state" is created, however, differed fundamentally between the Atlantic world and the Sahel. Hall shows how these differences came to be and how they were partly annulled by the colonial encounter. Although the book's main argument is one about the pre-colonial period, its main temporal focus remains on the nineteenth and twentieth centuries.

Hall has divided his book into four parts. These parts are not strictly chronological; they overlap in time frames, and are largely thematic. The first part discusses the construction of race from the first known historical sources on the subject from the fourteenth century until the nineteenth century in two chapters. The most important differences between race as it developed in Europe and the United States, and race as it was constructed in the Sahel, are the importance of genealogy and Islamic culture to define one's racial category as black or white. To be white in the Sahel today primarily means to have a recognized Arab or Berber ancestry and, from the point of view of those who define themselves as white, a more profound understanding of Islam, leading to better moral standards that justify political and economic dominance. These bases for racial discourse in the Sahel were put in place between the sixteenth and nineteenth centuries. A major departure from previous periods is the collapse of Arab and Berber ancestry into one white category, where previously these two were distinct. The second chapter continues to sketch how racial arguments were used juridically to defend the legal enslavement of black peoples.

Parts 2 and 3 focus on the colonial encounter in the Sahel in the nineteenth and early twentieth centuries, and the transformations of racial constructions in that period. These two parts, comprising five chapters, form the main body of the book. Hall does not argue that European notions of race did not have an impact on societies in the Sahel. He stresses the importance of a racial vision of Sahelian society that colonizer and colonized shared and which enabled both to understand the social and political processes that, together, they were shaping. In this process notions of race of the one influenced those of the other. To make this clear, Hall begins by sketching how the French vision of the Sahel became framed in racial notions, according to which the Tuareg were seen as a threat to colonial rule, while the Arab populations could be allies and the local black populations (in both French and Arab Berber eyes) were simply discarded as unimportant. He goes on to describe how colonizer and colonized used racial arguments to defend their positions toward each other. These negotiations involved the position of particular Tuareg and Arab lineages, and their economic and social hold over local sedentary black populations. Hall shows the extent to which a French racial discourse managed to superimpose itself by discussing how the French simply dismissed local Songhay and Fulani notions of their whiteness as nonsensical, and how racial notions of social political status and labor led to a collapse of various subordinate groups into one single category of slaves that was then internally redefined according to criteria the French supposed to be "traditional." This led to considerable redefinitions of both ethnic belonging and land ownership within the Niger bend that still play a major role today.

The last part, with one chapter, discusses the use of racial discourse and its alterations in the process of decolonization between 1940 and 1960. The foci of this chapter are the continued existence of slavery in the Niger bend in the middle of the twentieth century, which the French and the local white elite defended on the grounds of local racial specificities, and the emergence of local nationalist sentiments in the process of decolonization that became infused with a racial discourse on Saharan self and sub-Saharan other. The conclusion is not a classical résumé of what has been discussed previously, but rather an afterword in which Hall shows how what has been discussed throughout the book comes into play in the post-colonial period. However, it would have been more logical to simply include a slightly expanded version of this conclusion as a ninth chapter in part 4.

Hall's book is not about racial identities, or rather he states that he is not interested in identities per se, but in how racial arguments are "made to work" in particular social settings. However, the most specific way in which racial arguments are put to work is precisely in the construction of identities. It is therefore not surprising that much space remains devoted to the way Islamic scholars, inhabitants of the Niger bend, and the representatives of French colonial power used racial discourse to describe perhaps not the identity of particular peoples, but then at least their vision of them. Visions of the other influence visions of self, and what is identity other than perception? There is another reason why the formulation "putting to work" strikes me as somewhat evasive. Hall's reluctance to simply call his work an analytical deconstruction of discursive praxis is understandable, given the recent disregard for the tenets of postmodern academia, but unnecessary in his case. Most criticism of postmodern scholarship is not directed against its theoretical tenets or its methodology, but against the sloppy work that has been done in its name. However, the postmodern position against the uncritical acceptance of discursively structured power relations as "natural" remains an accepted stance. Given that racial discourse does exactly that—creating power relations through a discursive presentation of race as a "natural phenomenon"—an overt use of the postmodern methodological idiom would have been appropriate in this book, especially since Hall's work is anything but sloppy or excusatory. Quite the contrary.

What makes this work so outstanding is that it is for the larger part based on local Arabic source material, which ensures that the local visions of race and society are indeed local and not inferred through an interpretation of French source material. French archive material and literature are only used to give a French vision of the events when appropriate. The extensive use of Arabic source material not only means that Hall can make his primary arguments with sovereign authority—inter alia, most of the history of the French colonization of the Niger bend is being rewritten here through local eyes, which means that many previously received wisdoms need to be revised. For many of us, reading this book will mean reconsidering much of what we thought we knew about Islam, history, and society in the Sahel.

Baz Lecocq, Ghent University

Jonathon Glassman. *War of Words, War of Stones: Racial Thought and Violence in Colonial Zanzibar*. Bloomington: Indiana University Press, 2011. 398 pp., $80 hardcover, $30 paperback. Includes glossary and an index.

In December 1963 the islands of Zanzibar received their independence from the British colonizers. Within a month, in January 1964 the islands were rocked by a revolution that spawned racialized violence taking the lives of thousands of Arabs who lived in the islands. The racial politics of Zanzibar, which included African, Arab, and Indian communities, has intrigued scholars for decades. Jonathon Glassman's award-winning book (Martin Klein Prize from the American Historical Association, 2011) uses an analysis of race, ethnicity, and nationalism to explain the increasing levels of violence during the Time of Politics (1950s and 1960s) in Zanzibar. The book, which is divided into three sections, has eight chapters and an epilogue. The three sections focus on the "creation of race" and how it was deployed in Zanzibar, an analysis of race-making by the elite intelligentsia and subaltern intellectuals, and a study of crime, rumors, and violence surrounding the two elections of 1961. Glassman argues that by examining these elements we can see how the Revolution of 1964 and its attendant violence occurred.

The violence of and events leading up to the Zanzibar Revolution are generally framed as either a primordialist response to the oppression of the African population of the islands by Arabs or a reaction to the racialized colonial policies of the British. Glassman argues that neither is really the correct answer, as the racialized violence came out of the rhetoric of indigenous intellectuals and nationalist politicians. Rather than pinpoint the racialization of groups in the islands to a singular moment in time, he argues that race was constructed by a range of local actors. One of the significant theoretical contributions of the book is that it maps out the intellectual links between race, ethnicity, and nationalism. Glassman argues that these concepts are all based on "the metaphor of descent . . . that the peoples who are guardians of these discrete cultures are somehow linked by consanguinity." Thus race, ethnicity, and nationalism are all "modes of thought that fall toward opposing ends of a single continuum" but are clearly linked together (p. 11). "Racial thought," which he describes as "a shifting field of discourse: a general set of assumptions that humankind is divided among constituent categories, each of which is distinguished by inherited traits and characteristics," is created and re-created by competing groups in the islands. In the end, he argues that a paradigm that pits colonial thought against indigenous actions is useless; instead, he argues for a full analysis of the structure of local creations of race, ethnicity, and nationalism.

The second section of the book analyzes the ways in which both elite intelligentsia (read: the Zanzibar National Party) and subaltern nationalists (read: the Afro-Shirazi Party) created their own mythical histories of the islands. By drawing on the work of Randall Pouwels, Glassman demonstrates how the nineteenth-century coastal concept of *uungwana* defined islanders as "civilized" in contrast to the *ushenzi* or "barbarian-ness" of those from the African interior. Using this understanding of *uungwana*, which was later replaced by an Arabo-centric concept of *ustaarabu,* the book shows how the intelligentsia framed nation-building as "an act of uplift" that justified Arab dominance as more civilized than indigenous racial groups. In the final chapter of this section, the book illustrates how the racialized political speech of the intelligentsia and subalterns, as propagated through newspapers, was imbibed and filtered into the lives of ordinary Zanzibari citizens.

In the last section of the book Glassman uses the lens of rumors to demonstrate how violence becomes a "racial discourse." He traces how crime and racial politics became linked in the decades before the 1964 revolution. Accusations of crime were prevalent in the 1950s between landowners (read: Arabs) and squatters (read: Africans) who exchanged their labor for a small plot of land to use for themselves. Glassman defines these crimes as "social" crimes, which were conflicts based on customary understandings of patron-client relationships among landowners and squatters. This opened a space for people to reinterpret "crime" as a political action. Over time, particular groups gained reputations as criminally inclined. The WaManga (generally meaning recently migrated) Arabs and mainland ethnicities, especially the Wamakonde, were particularly suspect. Through rumor and fear, each group came to represent the criminal element of the racialized categories of Arab and African, respectively. As a result of the racialization of crime and rumors of crime, violence became a preemptive solution to fear and this violence helped to "reproduce racial discourse" (p. 230). Yet, in the end, violence or its extreme, genocide, are not inevitable. Racialized discourse offers the potential for violence, but it does not create the violence itself that must come from the will of individuals and collective groups of people.

The Revolution of 1964 lingers in the memory of Zanzibaris and continues to shape the ways in which Zanzibaris tell their history. Glassman is not the first scholar to note the difficulty of writing about the revolutionary period because of the way memories of the revolution shape present political discourse. In response to his concern about oral sources, he chose to focus solely on the abundant written documentation available from the era. His concerns are valid, yet his choices shape the book and discussion of race and identity in particular ways. Because women were not actively publishing and in the direct leadership of the various political parties of the 1950s, they are almost completely absent in this study. Yet the work of scholars such as Laura Fair in colonial Zanzibar and Susan Geiger in mainland Tanganyika demonstrates the active political roles women played within coastal society. Women received the vote in Zanzibar just in time for the elections of 1961, thus they were active participants in the events of the Time of Politics. It would be interesting to know how they were shaping racial discourse as well.

Many of the stories of rumors and threats of violence (such as the throwing of rocks at houses at night) are reminiscent of the practices of *uchawi* (witchcraft—for lack of a better translation). Glassman offers that rumors were at times fused with fears of *uchawi,* but he focuses on the idea of rumor rather than considering the ways in which *uchawi* signified power in Zanzibari communities. *Uchawi* was used throughout the colonial period as a means to demonstrate power and to discipline a variety of people: spouses, relatives, and colonial officials—both local and British, among others. Given the role of practitioners of *uchawi* as power brokers during the colonial era, the explicit violence of *uchawi* practices, and the implicit idea that it was "African" in origin, it seems striking that *uchawi* did not come up as a significant discussion in issues of race and violence during the Time of Politics.

This book is a well-researched and thorough history of the racial and nationalist discourse during the Time of Politics in the Zanzibar Islands. While it is written in a scholarly language, I have recommended it to advanced undergraduate students. It is highly recommended for graduate-level courses on race, nationalism, identity, politics, and Zanzibar.

Elisabeth McMahon, Tulane University

Janet McIntosh. *The Edge of Islam: Power, Personhood, and Ethno-Religious Boundaries on the Kenya Coast*. Durham, N.C.: Duke University Press, 2009, $94.95 hardcover, $24.95 paperback. 325 pages.

That margins are good to think upon has been a well-known truism in anthropology ever since the days of Victor Turner or Mary Douglas. Janet McIntosh has proved it once again by sitting at the edge of Islam to write up a very innovative ethnographic study of this religion, building upon an existing body of anthropological studies on Islam and on previous ethnographic and historical studies of coastal East Africa. Swahili and Giriama have been interacting (to some extent even intermarrying) along the coast for several centuries, living on the periphery of several Islamic worlds. But while Swahili-speaking individuals and groups make (increasingly greater) efforts to connect themselves to Arabic and Indian domains (and are perceived to be connected to them via their Muslim jinns or spirits by their neighboring Giriama), the latter fall out of the Muslim domain and maintain a very ambivalent relationship (indeed in some cases leading to madness) with this religious culture and with the hegemonic world of the Swahili. Today Giriama and Swahili perceive themselves as more and more different, and idioms of resentment and betrayal are often invoked to justify the ethnicized differences.

There are many reasons why I would consider this book a "must read" for students of religion in Africa. First, by focusing on such marginal dynamics and on the symbolic and economic exchanges between these two groups, it constitutes a very original study of Islam. Second, the study is achieved through a very skillful ethnography, one based on simultaneous fieldwork among the two linguistic groups, thus breaking the mono-ethnic approach of most ethnographic research carried out in Africa by a single person. Third, there is a potential dialogue with a very old tradition: the book addresses some classic issues of personhood, destiny, and intention that have informed anthropological debates in Africa since the days of our venerated ancestors to help us understand the internal differences between Giriama and Swahili religious cultures. Fourth, the book can be a very useful tool for those interested in what has become a common feature of the African landscape over the last twenty years: the political hardening of ethnic differences (often along religious lines) in areas that in the past had witnessed a much more fluid transformation of identities and a more positive set of exchanges. Fifth, the book will no doubt be read by scholars of religion interested in "syncretism." Rather than discussing whether the concept is useful or not to describe situations where religions meet, McIntosh invokes previous debates on syncretism to embark on a fascinating account of what she calls poly-ontology: the capacity some people have, in regions where religious cultures overlap, to switch from one ontology to another.

The historical dimension of the relationship between Swahili and Giriama along the coast is explained in chapter 1, which gives a diachronic depth (from pre-colonial to postcolonial politics, revisiting such important moments as the slave trade and colonial land policies) to issues later discussed in a more synchronic mode. The chapter helps explain the claim that today ethnicities are hardening while in the past they were much more fluid (even if we can see how a Swahili hegemony began to impose itself over other groups). Other chapters shed light on notions of personhood, belief, bodies, conversion, syncretism, and (one of my favorite parts of the study) the madness to which a fascination for Islam can lead among Giriama. McIntosh's approach to understanding how notions of personhood and internal attitudes and intentions shape different religious cultures, thus making it difficult for Giriama to convert to Islam (as it is lived by Swahili), is likely to inspire many other anthropologists working on religion and to enrich the burgeoning body of studies on Islam, belief, and prayer. The explanation, through poly-ontology, of how people live in such a constantly code-switching religious landscape is a valuable addition to the anthropological study of religious pluralism in sub-Saharan Africa.

Methodologically the book is exemplary. I wish more ethnographers, who normally focus on one ethnic group, could grasp the multicultural nature of their sites in a way similar to what McIntosh does. I also wish the attention to language and the dialogue with linguistic anthropology that she establishes were more common among ethnographers. Ethically speaking, the way she manages to echo voices from very distinct and competing points of view is also, I found, very tactfully and carefully achieved. The intermingling between theory (anthropology of Islam, notions of personhood, discussions on hegemony and ideology) and data is well achieved: the book becomes neither a hard read full of obscure theoretical lines nor a heavy ethnographic account, but rather a balanced study to be read with pleasure and profit.

All in all, I repeat, *The Edge of Islam* is a "must read" for anthropologists of religion in Africa. The book ends with a very useful epilogue in which the previous chapters are made relevant to understanding Kenyan politics at the time the book went into print. I for one would have preferred it to finish with a conclusion bringing the theoretical lines all together and helping us gauge the relevance of this study for the broader advance of anthropology and of religious studies. But this is of course a minor formal point, since readers will no doubt reach their own conclusion after reading these five fine and innovative chapters on the edge of Islam.

Ramon Sarró, University of Oxford